D0866165

Donated in memory of

Alixe Paisley

JULIA MARGARET CAMERON

Pioneer Photographer

Joy Melville

SUTTON PUBLISHING

> *For Ken*

First published in 2003 by
Sutton Publishing Limited · Phoenix Mill
Thrupp · Stroud · Gloucestershire · GL5 2BU

British Library Cataloguing in Publication Data
A catalogue record for this book is available from the British
Library.

ISBN 0-7509-3229-5

Typeset in 12/16 pt Perpetua.
Typesetting and origination by
Sutton Publishing Limited.
Printed and bound in England by
J.H. Haynes & Co. Ltd, Sparkford.

C O N T E N T S

LIST OF
ILLUSTRATIONS

ACKNOWLEDGEMENTS

A great many people have been very generous with their help and expertise. I am particularly grateful to Colin Ford, Violet Hamilton and Brian Hinton for the amount of time they have given me.

I would also like to thank Stuart Blake at the Royal Photographic Society, David Kuzma of Rutgers University Libraries, New Jersey, Pauline Melville, Richard Platt, Julia Rosenthal, Ron Smith, Chairman of the Dimbola Trust, Philippa Wright and Brian Liddy at the National Museum of Photography, Film & Television, Bradford, the staff of the Bodleian, British and London Libraries, the National Portrait Gallery, my agent Sara Menguc and my editor, Jaqueline Mitchell.

I am grateful to the following publishers for permission to use excerpts:

Hamish Hamilton for quotation from Wilfred Blunt's *England's Michelangelo: a Biography of George Frederic Watts*; to Special Collections and University Archives, Rutgers University Libraries, for access to Elizabeth Boyd's manuscript, 'The Pattle Sisters'; to the Society of Authors for quotation from Virginia Woolf's *Freshwater*; to Macmillan for quotation from Morton Cohen's *Lewis Carroll* and *The Letters of Lewis Carroll*; to Colin Ford for quotation from *The Cameron Collection*; to Hodder & Stoughton for quotation from Colin Gordon's *Beyond the Looking Glass*; to Violet Hamilton for quotation from *Annals of My Glasshouse*; to Peter Owen for quotation from Brian Hill's *Julia Margaret Cameron: A Victorian Family Portrait*; to Isle of Wight County Press and Isle of Wight County Council for quotation from Brian Hinton's *Immortal Faces* and to the Julia Margaret Cameron Trust for quotation from *Julia Margaret Cameron, Pioneer Victorian Photographer*; to Virago for quotation from Amanda Hopkinson's *Julia Margaret Cameron*; to Faber & Faber for quotation from Robert Bernard Martin's *Tennyson: The Unquiet Heart* and Ann Thwaite's *Emily Tennyson: The Poet's Wife*; to Random House Group for quotation from Tristram Powell (ed.) *Victorian Photographs of Famous Men and Fair Women*; to Routledge & Kegan Paul for quotation from Andrew Wheatcroft's *The Tennyson Album*.

I would like to thank the Royal Photographic Society for permission to reproduce the photograph of Ellen Terry. For all other photographs, I am indebted to the Wilson Centre for Photography.

Every effort has been made to trace copyright holders. Any errors or omissions are unintentional and will be corrected in future printings.

CHRONOLOGY

1815 Julia Margaret Pattle born at Garden Reach, Calcutta. Her parents were James and Adeline Pattle.

1818 Educated in Europe, in both London and Paris.

1834 Returns to Calcutta.

1838 Marries Charles Hay Cameron.

1839 Her first child, Julia, is born. Five sons were to follow.

1843 Cameron is appointed Member of the Council of India. He and his wife become leaders of Anglo-Indian society in Calcutta.

1847 Julia's translation of G.A. Burger's *Leonora* is published in London.

1848 The family returns to England on Charles Cameron's retirement and moves into a house at Tunbridge Wells, where their neighbour is poet Henry Taylor. Julia is a constant visitor at her sister, Sarah Prinsep's, artistic circle at Little Holland House. She meets the painter G.F. Watts and some Pre-Raphaelites, who are to influence her later photographic work.

1850 The Camerons follow the Taylors to London and move near them to Sheen Lodge, East Sheen.

Julia's friendship with Alfred and Emily Tennyson begins.

1857   A further move to Putney Heath. Mary Ryan, an attractive Irish beggar girl, approaches Julia, who takes her into her household and educates her alongside her own children. Mary later becomes her parlourmaid and model.

1860   The Camerons' coffee crop fails in Ceylon and Charles goes to investigate. While he is there, Julia buys two adjacent houses at Freshwater, Isle of Wight, next door to the Tennysons. She calls the property Dimbola. The family moves in.

1863   Julia is given a camera by her daughter, to alleviate her loneliness while her husband again visits Ceylon. She becomes a passionate photographer.

1864   Her photographs are shown at the Tenth Annual Exhibition of the Photographic Society, in London.

1865   Contributes to exhibitions in Scotland, Berlin and Dublin. Many critics are hostile, but at Berlin she is awarded the bronze medal. She mounts a one-woman show at Colnaghi's, Pall Mall, London.

1866   Exhibits again at Berlin and is awarded the gold medal. She has a further show at Colnaghi's and at the French Gallery, London. Adopts Cyllena,

Melita and Sheridan Wilson, the three orphaned children of the Camerons' friend the Revd Sheridan Wilson.

1867 Exhibits in Paris and receives an honourable mention.

1868 One-woman show at the German Gallery, London.

1873 Julia's daughter dies in childbirth. The lease of Little Holland House is up and the Prinseps and G.F. Watts decide to move to the Isle of Wight.

1874 She starts work on illustrations for the first volume of the Cabinet edition of Tennyson's *Idylls of the King*. Disappointed with the reduced size of the photographs, she publishes her own version, with twelve large photographs.

1875 Writes a fragment of her autobiography, *Annals of My Glasshouse*, which is not published until 1889. She starts work on the second volume of *Idylls of the King*. In October the Camerons leave England to join their sons in Ceylon. From then on Julia only photographs occasionally.

1878 They return for a month's holiday in England.

1879 Julia dies on 26 January at her son's house in the mountains of Ceylon and is buried in St Mary's churchyard, Bogawantalawa.

1880 Charles Cameron dies and is buried next to his wife.

INTRODUCTION

The casual gift of a camera from her daughter in 1863 transformed Julia Margaret Cameron's life. She was forty-eight years old and until then her ferocious energy had no real outlet. She took up photography with a passion, breaking the mould of the conventional stiff Victorian portraiture and elevating photography to a high art with her allegorical, biblical and literary images. Her photographic studies, particularly those of 'Famous Men and Fair Women', had a powerful and arresting intensity which outshone other contemporary portraits.

However, her originality, her deliberate and dreamlike soft-focus technique, her dramatic use of lighting and her pictorial imagery, aroused waspish hostility. The *Photographic News*, in reviewing an exhibition of hers in 1868, said: 'Not even the distinguished character of some of the heads serve, however, to redeem the result of wilfully imperfect photography from being altogether repulsive . . .'.

She aroused anger among male photographers by daring to compete professionally with them in an age when women were expected to dabble prettily in the arts but not to challenge the accepted male supremacy.

Nevertheless, she did have male admirers including Victor Hugo, who wrote: 'No one has ever captured the rays of the sun and used them as you have. I throw myself at your feet.'

She herself shrugged off her critics, confidently organised exhibitions of her photographs, and worked and networked frenetically. She cajoled and bullied her sitters, once leaving Robert Browning posing for two hours while she hunted for some missing equipment. When illustrating Tennyson's Arthurian tales, *Idylls of the King*, she ruthlessly commandeered as a model any passer-by who possessed the face she wanted, and rarely did a potential subject escape.

The seeds of her photographic talent were already evident in her character. She was a formidable, feisty woman. Plain in appearance, she had imaginative curiosity, exceptional verve and drive, steely determination and overwhelming confidence. Yet despite her bohemian, unorthodox behaviour, she also played the role of conventional Victorian wife and upheld many of the ideals of the mid-Victorian age. Born in Calcutta in 1815, she was educated in Europe before returning to India and, at twenty-three, marrying Charles Hay Cameron, a distinguished civil servant twenty years her senior. She became Calcutta's leading hostess, ran the household and produced six children.

Her life changed when her husband retired and the family came to England in the late 1840s. She became part of a literary and artistic circle based at her sister Sarah's home, Little Holland House, in London. It included nearly everyone of talent in Victorian London, from Thackeray to Ellen Terry, Carlyle to Rossetti. Many of those she met there she was later to photograph.

She and her husband and family later moved to the Isle of Wight, next door to her dear friend, Tennyson. It was there that Julia Margaret Cameron took up photography. For twelve years she worked furiously – an exceptionally short time for the extraordinary body of work she produced. Then, in 1875, aged sixty, she ungrudgingly gave it all up to accompany her husband to Ceylon (Sri Lanka), an island he loved and where he owned large coffee estates. Her sons were working there and she was to say, 'Where your heart is, there is your treasure also.' She photographed relatively rarely after that and, three years later, while staying with one of her sons in the mountains of Ceylon, she died.

Her vision and artistic treatment were to influence generations of future photographers. Yet after her death astonishingly little attention was paid to her work. Only through dedicated Cameron scholars were her photographs re-evaluated and shown in various exhibitions, allowing their brilliance to be seen once again.

CALCUTTA DAYS

Calcutta in 1815, where Julia Margaret was born, was a splendid place for the affluent, with its dazzlingly colourful flowers and birds; palatial residences, horse races and cricket matches, picnics and balls, water parties and garden parties, and nightly sunset carriage parades, where the fashionable acknowledged each other on Calcutta's Esplanade.

Julia was one of seven daughters born to James and Adeline Pattle. Adeline, a beautiful and graceful woman, came from a good family. Her father was the Chevalier de l'Etang, a courtier at Versailles during the reign of King Louis XVI and Queen Marie Antoinette. According to some accounts, he took rather too much interest in the Queen, and was posted out to Pondicherry in French India. There he met and married Thérèse Blin de Grincourt, a one-time maid of honour to Marie Antoinette and renowned for her beauty. He held various responsible posts there but family tradition has it that the couple returned to Paris and the Chevalier was with Marie Antoinette when she was imprisoned and guillotined in 1793. He and his wife left – promptly – for India and by 1800 were established in Calcutta.

When the Chevalier died, or so it is romantically claimed, a miniature of Marie Antoinette was buried with him. His wife returned to France and lived at Versailles until her death in 1866 at ninety-eight years.[1]

One of their daughters, Adeline de l'Etang, who had inherited her mother's beauty – as indeed future generations were to do – married an Englishman, James Pattle, in 1811. Born in Bengal, though educated in London, James was accepted into the Bengal civil service at the age of sixteen in 1791.[2] He was steadily promoted to more senior administrative and judicial posts. At the time of his marriage to Adeline – when he was a judge at the provincial court of Murshidabad on the River Ganges – he was a rich, highly placed civil servant. He appeared to be a pillar of society, but was dubbed by his enemies as 'the biggest liar in India'. His friends regarded him as a bon vivant and generous host who could be relied on to offer excellent claret and tip-top champagne.

The couple's first daughter, also called Adeline, was born in 1812. That year James was transferred to Calcutta and it was there that Julia was born, on 11 June 1815. She was the couple's fourth child. Sadly for them, their one son had died the year of his birth (1813) and their next daughter only lived until she was four. Adeline was to have six more daughters: Sarah (1816), Maria (1818), Louisa (1821), Virginia (1827), Harriet (1828, died the same year) and, last of all, Sophia (1829).

James and Adeline and their family lived in an impressive residence in an area called Garden Reach on the bank of the River Hooghli, a few miles outside Calcutta. Large houses in that district in those days were raised on a basement some 18 ft high which contained the kitchen, bathroom, storerooms and spare rooms. The reception rooms and the best bedrooms would be in the upper part of the house. Green venetian blinds would give protection from the sun, while broad verandahs overlooked the river. These gave splendid views of the grounds, most of which were 'shaded by the boughs of blossoming mango trees and the spreading banyan'.[3]

The children of Anglo-Indian families in those days were usually taken by their mother or nurse to Europe from the age of three years upwards. There they stayed until they were eighteen or nineteen. Their educational opportunities there were far better than any schooling they could expect in India and it was a healthier climate than the hot sun and fevers of India.

This meant, for the mother, frequent and tedious five- or six-month voyages to and from India, round the coast of Africa via the Cape of Good Hope, when violent storms could practically upend the ship. Indeed, one of the Pattle children, aged four, died at sea: another was born at sea. Adeline took her children to France in turn to the care of her mother, Madame de l'Etang, in Versailles, and also to London. Adeline and her sisters had been educated in Paris at a select private school run in those days by a Mrs Campan, a friend of their mother. The Pattle girls may have attended the same school — though, as an adult, Sarah used to complain that she had had no education at all.

Julia was taken to Europe by her mother as a very young child of about three or four years old, around 1818, staying there until she was nineteen. Like her sisters, she was educated in London and Paris. It is a hazy, virtually undocumented period. There are no descriptions of Julia as a child, what schools she went to, or how long she remained in each respective country. But she and her sisters all spent their holidays with their grandmother in Versailles and enjoyed this immensely when they were young. Life for them there was untrammelled — in one of the few remarks she made to a friend about her childhood, Julia said she and her sister Sarah 'used to wander forth and kneel and pray on the country roadsides'. Madame de l'Etang was unperturbed by this. It was said she 'solved the problem of education for her granddaughters by having them taught all sorts of housewifely arts, rather to the neglect of lesson-books and accomplishments'.[4] In line with current thinking, girls were expected to concentrate on making a successful, hopefully brilliant, marriage. Being able to cook, sew and entertain was much more use than a classical education.

The girls' aunts — their mother's two sisters, Mrs Edward Impey and Mrs Samuel Beadle — were also

4

living in France. While the children were growing up in France, they and their mother, aunts and grandmother often entertained other Anglo-Indian families like the Thackerays. William Makepeace Thackeray also met the Pattle family in London in the early 1830s, as well as in Versailles and Paris. He was particularly taken with the 'ravishing' good looks of the daughters. He pursued the acquaintance and in 1833 wrote wistfully to his mother, saying if only one of the elder daughters had a fortune to match her face, he'd marry her out of hand. Julia did not share in the dazzling looks of her sisters – though her sister Sarah was comely rather than beautiful – but she made an impression on him and in later years in England he brought his daughters to meet her.

Whenever the girls' mother was away on these long trips to Europe, their father, James Pattle, reverted to bachelor behaviour. He was an energetic, influential figure in Calcutta, but lived up to his reputation of being a rogue. Ethel Smyth, the composer, remembered the evening when her father, who had been on the Governor General's staff in Calcutta and knew James well, started to reminisce about him. She said her father remembered him as being 'as big a scamp as ever you saw, and a bad fellow in every way. Behaved very ill to his wife too, but she was devoted to him and when – well, when anything went wrong, he used to say that it *couldn't be helped now* and she was quite satisfied and forgave him again and again.'[5]

Julia returned to India from Europe in 1834, when she was nineteen, to take her part in the social life in Calcutta. There was a shortage of English girls in Calcutta then – indeed at one Government House party two gentlemen had to take in each lady. Another time, one hostess could only muster sufficient dancing partners for sixteen young men. Although soldiers may have looked attractive in their uniform, worldly mothers pointed out firmly to their daughters that a civil servant, with his chances of promotion, was a far better marital prospect.

Julia was not someone who would have been swept off her feet by mere good looks and a uniform. She had a very quick mind, definite ideas and a wide range of interests – preferring a discussion on literature to social chit-chat. Although the family was well off and she would have been regarded as a catch, her looks were not prepossessing. She had penetrating, sharp, dark eyes, a sallow complexion and a wart on her face. Her figure was also inclined to be dumpy. But then, and for the whole of her life, she was generous, unconventional, loyal and unpredictable.

Her health was not very good – she was prone to respiratory infections – and when she was twenty-one, she had a bout of illness and was sent to the Cape of Good Hope, South Africa, with its more refreshing climate, to recuperate. There she met two men, one of whom she married, while the other, Sir John Herschel, became her mentor. Herschel was an English astronomer who pioneered celestial photography, carried out research on photo-active chemicals, and for relaxation translated from *The Iliad*. In 1834 he had installed an observatory in the Cape to survey the sky of the southern hemisphere.

The other man was Charles Hay Cameron who, like Julia, had gone to the Cape to recuperate. Cameron, born in 1795, was a widower and at forty-one was twenty years older than Julia. He was recovering from an exhausting spell of work in Calcutta where he had been working with Macaulay on writing the Indian Penal Code, a code of criminal law. He was of aristocratic lineage. His mother, Lady Margaret Hay, was a daughter of the Earl of Errol, and his father – descended from the Jacobite, Archibald Cameron of Lochiel – was Governor of Malta, and of the Bahamas.

The three – Cameron, Julia and Herschel – remained close, keeping up an intellectual friendship, sending books to each other and exchanging critical comments on them. They were all interested in the arts: Julia translated, and had published, Gottfried August Burger's poem *Leonora*. Herschel kept them informed about the latest scientific discoveries, including those to do with photography. When Julia herself became a photographer, many years later in 1863, this background and Herschel's knowledge, were invaluable to her.

On 1 February 1838, two years after they met, Charles Cameron and Julia married in Calcutta.

Apart from the two youngest sisters, Virginia and Sophia, all the other Pattle sisters married during the 1830s and all married well. The same year as Julia married Cameron, Louisa married Henry Bayley who was to become Judge of the Supreme Court in Calcutta. A third sister, Maria, had married the highly respected Dr John Jackson in 1835 – the same year that a fourth sister, Sarah, married Thoby Prinsep, a high-ranking administrator.

TWO

'MY LOVED CHARLES'

Charles and Julia lived in Calcutta for the next ten years, until 1848. Despite their age difference, the marriage was exceptionally happy. Their relationship was long-lasting and fundamental. They both admired each other intellectually, were enthusiastic and involved in the arts and were erudite and witty conversationalists. Charles, who fired in Julia his own interest in philosophy and classical literature, was an imaginative and profound thinker with a list of impressive achievements to his credit.

Although Thomas Carlyle wrote rather disparagingly of him that he had 'a sleek small red face, lively little black eyes, and no *chin* to speak of'[1] this was merely a personal observation and one of the few adverse comments about him. Sir Henry Cotton wrote approvingly of Cameron as being 'one of the most distinguished-looking men I have ever met. His words were always wise'.[2] The poet Sir Henry Taylor was to write an admiring testimonial for him, praising his high intellectual power and saying he was 'an accomplished

Scholar and Gentleman of great literary and general knowledge and his writings are in grace, force and clearness of diction, superior to almost any of his time'.[3]

Charles had a respected work pedigree. After being called to the Bar in England, he went to Ceylon to investigate its judicial procedure, publishing his official report in 1832. He took such a strong liking to the island that he bought extensive coffee estates there. He believed strongly that law and education would create liberty for Ceylon's population and the 1833 Ceylon Charter of Justice was his work. That year he sat on the Committee of the Society for the Diffusion of Useful Knowledge, publishers of the *Penny Magazine*.

Cameron cared deeply about education and what direction this should take under colonial rule and to that end became a member – then President – of the Council of Education for Bengal (later called the Council of India). He believed that education ought to be in accordance with British standards, and proposed that English be the language used in higher education. His work in Calcutta led to the formation of its university. He was to work with Macaulay in Calcutta on the Penal Code. A reformer, he was one of the last disciples of the philosopher Jeremy Bentham.

In 1838, at twenty-three, Julia became pregnant with her first child. She was so delighted she wrote a long, heartfelt prayer of thanks. The child, born the following year, was a daughter, called Julia after her mother. She was the couple's only – and naturally adored – daughter. Five sons followed: Eugene Hay; Ewen W. Hay; Hardinge Hay; Charles Hay and Henry Herschel (called after the couple's old friends, Henry Taylor and Sir John Herschel).

Julia was a devoted mother and in true Victorian tradition produced a child every two years or so. She loved her children and spent as much time as she could with them, though she followed the convention of sending them to England when they were very young. Unlike her own mother she did not take them herself but sent them with a nurse, as she considered it her duty to stay and help her husband. Her grandmother's training upheld, for she successfully acted as social and political hostess to Charles, entertaining everyone of note in Calcutta with panache.

Emily Eden, who was in India from 1836 to 1842 when her brother George, the 2nd Baron Auckland, was Governor General there, was fiercely scathing about Calcutta society then, finding it 'detestable'. She thought it highly formal and a positively suffocating form of exile, dubbing the society there as second-rate and condemning the few topics discussed by the Anglo-Indians.[4]

Julia's letters show that she had an interest in politics outside Calcutta. A good friend of Julia and Charles, a Major Broadfoot, kept her up to date with the situation where he was stationed in Tulalabad. Writing in 1842, he tells her he can't forward her package to 'poor Colin' [the Colin Mackenzie once married to her oldest sister Adeline, who had died at sea in 1836] as he was the prisoner of Muhammad Phah Khan, a few miles west of Kabul. However, he had sent him a message to say that Lord Ellenborough had referred all the papers regarding the Kabul affairs to Mr Cameron for a report. In his opinion, no Governor General since Warren Hastings had faced such difficulties as Lord Ellenborough. Never since Clive had there been 'such deficiency of equipment in our armies with such want of energy and resource in those who ought to set matters right'.[5]

She regarded the political scene with a certain amused cynicism. She wrote to Major Broadfoot, in September 1843, to say 'The Council has a very meagre aspect (not meagre in the literal acceptance of the word for the Depy. Gov. alone, always a Falstaffian appearance, is now so blown out with the dignity of his position that he might represent a whole body of men.)... Lord Ellenboro', if it be not treason to say so is flighty & unmanageable in all matters of business, shrewd eno' but wholly without ballast.'[6]

That same year, 1843, Charles was appointed the first legal Member of the Council of India. It was the highest of posts. As, over the next five years under the Governor Generalships of Lords Ellenborough and Dalhousie, there were no official 'Governor General Ladies' this role, in effect, fell to Julia. Henry Taylor, an administrator in the

Colonial Office, a writer and a good friend of the Camerons, told a friend that she was now the head of the European society. Julia took to the role effortlessly and led Calcutta society in its round of dinners, receptions and balls. Invitations to the Camerons' home were eagerly sought after: everyone was aware of the hosts' hospitality and witty, learned conversation.

Julia's letter to Major Broadfoot that year gave him an insight into the rushed life she and Charles were leading and revealed her consistently strong support for and concern about her husband. Although she describes with pleasure the decorative scene of the Calcutta ballrooms, which she attributes to the number of men in brightly coloured uniforms, she invariably returns to her husband's situation. His position, she admitted, 'is not a comfortable or a fair one', and claimed there were few men there whose minds were liberal enough to understand her husband's 'large views' of matters.

The decision that had been facing the couple that year – 1843 – was whether they stayed in India or returned to England. Julia went on to tell Major Broadfoot that Charles's friends were currently entreating him to stay in Calcutta and work out his reforms until they had been completed. But these same friends, she pointed out, forgot that he was powerless without support and that 'while he is sacrificing in this vile climate the best years of his life and devoting his best intellect and best energies, he is doing no good at all'.

Lively and active, with a powerful personality, Julia was nevertheless careful, in accordance with the conventions of the time, not to let her views prevail. As she told Major Broadfoot, 'I have never sought to persuade or bias my loved Charles either in favour of going home or remaining here. With so little ambition as he has, with so much taste for literary leisure and retired life, I think he would be far happier at home but he might think he was wasting abilities that he ought to have devoted to public life and public good.' She considered that no wife should let 'the devotedness of her love' push her husband into a decision about which he had a shadow of doubt.[7] In her case, she channelled her energy instead into various activities. One of the most spectacular of these was raising the immense sum of £14,000 to help the Irish during their great famine of the 1840s.

Julia was twenty-eight in 1843 and was longing to return to England (it was still five years before her wish came true). One reason for this was 'my boy's departure'. She was following tradition by sending her children to England for their education. As a devoted mother as well as wife, she told Major Broadfoot that year that she had been very anxious about her son, Eugene. He was on his way to England by ship and had been ill. The ship had put into Mauritius for water and she had just heard from the nurse that he had recovered and was the pet of the ship. She wrote joyously about this and of her adored four-year-old daughter. ('My Julia is in the most perfect health and becomes more engaging every day.') She was pregnant again at the time and though admitting she was spending far too much of her care and tenderness on Julia, believed this would change after the arrival of her new baby in December 1843.

Despite her fervent wish that all the family should remain under one roof, her sense of duty was strong. In the same letter to Major Broadfoot, she wrote: 'I do not sacrifice so much as does my loved Husband for he has the toils and trammels of office to endure and therefore I only pray that so long as he stays my health may enable me to remain also.' She was worried about the effect of the hot climate on him and when she went to balls, she went without her husband. 'The heat of a ballroom in the month of September in Calcutta is so trying that it would knock anyone up who could not make the succeeding day a day of rest, and this he never is able to do.'[8]

Her resolution to stay in India almost failed her, making her ill, when Julia, then six, was due to be sent to England. She had been upset at the thought for some time, writing to Broadfoot on 6 December 1844 to say it was her precious Julia's birthday, the last one she would spend in India ('what that thought brings to my heart you who know my heart can know & tell').[9] Charles wrote to Broadfoot on 9 February 1845 to say his wife was suffering from a feverish attack, brought on, he thought, by longing for her absent daughter. Julia added a postscript, an outpouring of some ten pages to say she hadn't written 'for fear of opening afresh those channels of grief'.

As one of her friends said, Julia alternated between the seventh heaven and the bottomless pit: 'she lives upon superlatives as upon her daily bread'. Reading what she writes, one could be forgiven for imagining that her daughter had died, rather than sailed away, as she refers to the 'great loss' of her beloved child, the darling of her heart. She says that 'she never was one hour out of my sight, never slept out of my room' and describes at length the anguish of the hour of parting, when even her husband wept sorely, and the final return to the house 'where she was to be seen no more and heard no more'. Although she admits she has her small son Ewen to console her at home, she says she is now 'raising a sort of bulwark round one's heart' to avoid future suffering when he in turn has to leave. Not even knowing that in England her darling would encounter 'green fields and a feeling of health and vigour' made up for life without her.

One would have thought that she might have kept her children, or at least her daughter, in India to avoid all this anguish, but she explained this by her remark that 'a strong sense of duty of having in plain words done what was right to be done, still consoles me . . . the setting aside of every human feeling and thinking only of her permanent good'.[10] Both Julia's daughter and her younger brother Eugene were to make their home with Charles Cameron's sister, in Worthing, between 1845 and 1847.

Charles and Julia's social stature enabled them to overcome the gossip surrounding Julia's father, James Pattle, when he finally drank himself to death in 1845. It was discovered, to everyone's surprise, that he had left instructions for his body be embalmed and buried next to his mother in the family vault at Marylebone church in London. James's friends were amused by this, but respected the decision of his widow, Adeline, that her husband's wishes must be carried out. Their way of 'embalming' the body was to preserve it in a cask of spirits. The story goes that once the cask and its contents were ready to be shipped off to England, Adeline insisted on having it placed in a spare room next to her bedroom until the vessel was ready to take him. In the middle of the night there was a loud explosion. Adeline rushed into the room and found the cask had burst . . . 'and there was her husband half out of it'!

His friends still thought they should carry out James's last wishes, even if the build-up of gases caused another explosion, so his body was put inside a new cask and was shipped down the Ganges on its way to England. Ethel Smyth's father reported that, 'The sailors hadn't the most distant idea who they'd got on board, and thinking the cask was full of rum, which was the case, they tapped it and got drunk and, by Jove, the rum ran out and got alight and set the ship on fire! And while they were trying to extinguish the flames she ran on a rock, blew up, and drifted ashore just below Hooghly. And what do you think the sailors said? That Pattle had been such a scamp that the Devil wouldn't let him out of India!'[11] The story was such a good one that different versions proliferate. One has it that, after a storm, the cask broke open and 'Mr Pattle was standing up in it, grim and terrible'.

What was perhaps most typical of James Pattle was that a letter eventually came from the rector of Marylebone church to say that the Pattles had never had a vault in his church. However, despite these penny-dreadful stories about the aftermath of James's death, his body did ultimately reach England (though whether in a cask of spirits or not isn't known) and was buried in St Giles church, Camberwell.

Smyth claimed that the shock of discovering her dead husband half out of the cask sent Adeline Pattle off her head and that she 'died raving', but this wasn't so. Understandably, she did become very ill with the shock but in the December of that same year, 1845, she forced herself to accompany her two younger unmarried daughters, Virginia and Sophia, on a boat bound for England. Her intention was to take the girls to stay with their older married sister, Sarah, who with her husband and family was now living in London.

Adeline contemplated the voyage with apprehension, which was hardly surprising as she was far from well. She had also been upset by her eldest daughter, another Adeline, dying at sea quite recently at the age of thirty-four while on a voyage to restore her health after being seriously weakened by the birth of her third child. If Adeline Pattle did have a premonition, she was sadly proved right. The ship had hardly left the harbour before she, too, succumbed to her ill health and died. The two orphaned girls, Virginia and Sophia, only eighteen and sixteen years old respectively, had no option but to continue their journey to stay with their sister, Sarah, in London.

They showed the resilience, determination and individuality which characterised all the redoubtable Pattle family. Indeed, Lord Dalhousie said that he divided mankind into 'Men, women and Pattles'.

The agonising separation of Julia from her children did not come to an end for a further three years. But in 1848 Charles Cameron finally decided to retire. He was fifty-three and his wife was thirty-three. The plan was that he would devote his time to classical studies and the family would live on the proceeds of the coffee estates that he had bought in Ceylon years ago. At last they were able to head for London and join Julia's other sisters who were already living there: Sarah, Virginia, Sophia, Maria and Louisa.

THREE

THE HOLY SISTERHOOD

London in the early 1840s was a city of bustling change. Queen Victoria had only been on the throne since 1837, but the thrust of modernisation had begun. Euston and London Bridge stations had opened in 1837, the penny post was introduced in 1840 and Thomas Cook organised his first excursion holiday in 1841. The tax on glass was lifted in 1845, leading to a fast rise in the number of conservatories, and Harrods opened in 1849. Everyone was adapting to a new way of life: etiquette books, for instance, had to give advice on how to wrestle correctly with railway luggage.

In those days it was usual to rent property, not buy. Around the mid-nineteenth century, rent for one room was about £5 a year, rising to about £50 for a ten-roomed house. No one wanted fitted carpets as this was a needless extravagance when one might move six months later. Instead, Turkey rugs covered the floor and Oriental carpets masked the table. There were potted palms, patterned flock wallpaper and paintings of stags at bay or ships in storms. A battery of maids polished brasswork, cleaned grates, scrubbed and dusted. For this reason servants were crucial. In the 1840s, it was estimated one needed an income of £150 a year to cover household expenses and a servant. To hire just one to come in and clean cost £3 a year, while a resident maid would be £9 a year.

The Pattle sisters, married and single, had first started to converge on London in 1843, five years before the Camerons arrived in England. That year Sarah, Julia's younger sister by a year, together with her husband, Thoby Prinsep, and their family of three boys and one girl, returned from India to England. They rented a house at 9 Chesterfield Street, near Berkeley Square. Sarah, the most maternal of the sisters, also provided a home there for another sister, Maria or 'Mia' as she was known to the family. Maria had married Dr John Jackson, a leading doctor in Calcutta, beloved by his patients and totally immersed in his practice. But her health was poor and she left her husband for the cooler climate of England. Only on his retirement, seven years later, did he join her.

Maria wrote to Julia in Calcutta in 1843, while staying with Sarah, to tell her that her health and spirits were now improving. Julia was delighted to hear that Maria was 'leading as ever a tranquil domestic life, being loved and admired'. In the September of that year Julia told her friend Major Broadfoot that though every mail from England brought news from the Prinseps, 'they are not such satisfactory accounts as we could wish. My sister Sarah mistaking real happiness for that which has at best but its semblance and which to me has not even that to recommend it has launched forth at once into fashionable London life.'

It was not that Julia disapproved of fashionable life as such, but in Sarah's case, she told Major Broadfoot, she 'meets with const. disappt. from the worldliness, the pride and the arrogance of those in whose circle she moves, yet she has not the courage to renounce at once all these vanities and to come out from amongst them. I hope however one season in London will sicken her so that she will after that live amongst those whose real feelings are more congenial to her own.'[1]

In 1845, two years after the Prinseps came to London, the young Virginia and Sophia arrived there after the traumatic sea voyage during which their mother had died. They went straight to live with Sarah and Thoby at their house in Chesterfield Street. The Prinseps were comfortably off and had no problem in supporting the sisters. Like Julia, Sarah had married a man twice her age: she was just nineteen in 1835, at the time of her wedding to Thoby Prinsep in India, while her husband was forty-three. He was a distinguished figure in the Indian Civil Service and had been very rich out there, but had then lost a large sum of money standing unsuccessfully for Parliament. After some thirty-five years of administration in India, he had retired and returned to England and was now a Member of Council at the India Office.

Thoby didn't appeal to everyone. One of the sisters of Lord Auckland, who had been a Governor General of India, wrote in her journal that Thoby was 'the greatest bore Providence ever created, and so contradictory that he will not let anyone agree or differ with him'.[2] But an English admirer was the painter G.F. Watts, who considered him a positive encyclopedia of valuable information on every sort of subject and that talking to him was just like turning the pages of a delightful book. Some *Punch*-minded readers in England facetiously referred to him as Sarah's 'Dog Thoby'.

In writing about the seven Pattle sisters, Wilfrid Blunt, the biographer of G.F. Watts, said they sounded like a turn in the big tent and that there was something decidedly theatrical about them. They bought a new dimension to the Victorian cultural scene – enlivening it and unhesitatingly flouting convention if it suited them, as they were to do all their lives.

Within a few years of the sisters arriving, they were known as the 'holy sisterhood' – and were bywords in London. Anne Thackeray, the writer's daughter and later Lady Ritchie, said of them, 'They were unconscious artists with unconventional rules for life which excellently suited themselves.'[3] Virginia was famous for her beauty, Sarah for her salons and her cook, Sophia was beloved for her goodness, while Maria encompassed most of her sisters' virtues – with the added plus, through her daughter's second marriage to Leslie Stephen, of ultimately becoming grandmother to Virginia Woolf and Vanessa Bell.

Bright, original and unaware of their eccentricities, all the sisters stood out from the crowd. They were devoted to each other and their memories of India brought them even closer. One friend said that among themselves in London they talked in Hindustani and that 'this seemed to an outsider the language best suited to express their superabundant vitality'. All of them were artistic and shared a love of beauty, which their clothes emphasised. They preferred to design these themselves and the rich colour and ample folds were simple, striking and individual. Lady Somerset remembered that when they all met, they sat up all night in an orgy of dressmaking, 'pulling their robes to bits and sewing them up in a new way . . . they scorned Fashion, wore neither crinoline nor stays, and in long flowing garments designed and made by themselves, they walked serenely like goddesses through the London streets'. They preferred cloaks to crinolines and one wore 'a scarlet Turkey-twill toga bound with dull gold braid over an olive-green soft satin under-robe with puffed sleeves and an Indian shawl trailing over all'.[4] When Julia joined them from India in 1848, she was seen clad in 'silken folds and glittering decoration . . . confronted the common world of convention and habit, not only unrestrained by its normal boundaries, but unconscious of their very existence'.[5]

Lady Somerset considered that the three sisters, Virginia, Sarah and Julia, were a blend of both their parents – 'passionate, wilful, "headstrong as a Pattle", brilliant or beautiful, everything in their nature, even their mother's sensitiveness and imaginativeness seems to have been touched by the "blazing" quality of their father'.[6] 'Pattledom' passed into the language of the mid-nineteenth century. Virginia, Sarah and Julia were to be nicknamed 'Beauty, Dash and Talent' respectively. Julia's 'talent' was to come later, with her unmatched, striking photography. When she first arrived – a rather squat, dark-haired and forceful woman – she, like Sarah, cut more of a 'Dash'.

Despite Julia's once-expressed hope that Sarah's socialising would sicken her, her time in London had only whetted Sarah's social appetite and she had become a celebrity lion-hunter. Her one ambition was to establish her house as a literary and artistic salon. She was indefatigable (but successful) in chasing down everyone of note.

In 1847, just before the Camerons arrived, she had met the painter G.F. Watts through her sister, Virginia, who was still living with Sarah in London. Sophia had left that year to marry Sir John Warrender Dalrymple. Watts had passed Virginia in the street and been struck by her beauty and the elegance of the long grey cloak she was wearing, which fell in folds against her tall figure. He quickly manoeuvred an introduction to paint her and Virginia brought Sarah along as chaperone. Unknown at that time to Watts, Sarah was to dominate his life for the next thirty years.

Virginia was the acknowledged beauty of the family. Although all the sisters, with the exception of Julia, had above average good looks, Virginia was ravishing. After one ball she went to, she received sixteen proposals and once such a large crowd collected outside an Oxford Street store she had entered that she had to leave by a side door. Thackeray penned a verse to her in *Punch* but she herself was irritated by the reaction to her loveliness. Once, on receiving an ode to her beauty, she read it and burst into tears, saying 'They all say that, nothing but that.'[7] Watts painted her several times – one study was so small that Julia used to carry it around inside her watch case – and the romantic story goes that Viscount Eastnor (later the Earl of Somers) saw one of Watts's portraits of Virginia in the Academy Exhibition of 1849 and immediately decided to marry her. Fortunately for him she agreed and they married the following year.

Sarah, meanwhile, was delighted to meet Watts. In her eyes (and his) he was a neglected genius and she gave him a standing invitation to come to their house in Chesterfield Street. He had just returned from staying with Lord and Lady Holland in Florence so had, to

Sarah, the added advantage of being able to bring in a circle of artistic and social contacts through the Hollands.

With such possibilities ahead, Sarah felt the house at Chesterfield Street, although several storeys high, was too cramped to entertain distinctive guests and began looking around for a more distinguished property. Watts suggested to her that she should consider leasing Little Holland House in Kensington from Lord Holland. It was a large, rambling dower house on the Holland estate, with a thatched porch, gabled roof and long corridors inside leading to rooms of different heights and strange shapes. It was only two miles from Hyde Park but it was romantically rural, with long green lawns, meadows and a croquet ground, and the Prinseps were delighted with it. In 1850 they signed a 21-year lease. Sarah, in an attempt to rescue Watts's spirits from one of his constant fits of melancholia, persuaded him to come and stay there. That, with Watts, was a mistake. He had irritated Lord and Lady Holland by extending his visit to them to four years and ignoring hints to leave, and he behaved in exactly the same way with the Prinseps. As Sarah was to say ruefully at one point, 'He came to stay three days – he stayed 30 years.'

However, she cosseted him and, as George Frederic Watts was not the type of man to call George or Fred, referred to him as 'Signor'. She showed off her trophy at her bohemian Sunday tea parties where guests ate strawberries and cream in the garden, strolled around the rambling gardens, played croquet or went to Watts's vast studio and admired his canvases. When the young actress Ellen Terry – later to marry Watts – first went there, she was captivated by the spacious rooms, the series of wall frescoes by Watts, how all the men were gifted, all the women graceful.

The house was visited by practically every creative person of note during the 1850s and 1860s, such as the writers Charles Dickens, George Meredith, Tom Hughes, Thomas Carlyle, George Eliot, Edward Bulwer-Lytton, Coventry Patmore, John Ruskin and William Thackeray; the poets Alfred Tennyson, Henry Taylor and the Brownings; the sculptor and poet Thomas Woolner, and the painters Dante Gabriel Rossetti, John Everett Millais, Edward Burne-Jones, Frederick Leighton and Holman Hunt. Disraeli and Gladstone were occasional visitors along with the illustrator Richard Doyle, whose cover design for *Punch* in January 1849 remained unchanged for over a century. Sarah, like Julia, was an acclaimed hostess. Guests were serenaded by piano and cello and the musician Joseph Joachim played the violin.

Julia herself was a regular guest. Watts's second wife Mary, in discussing the habitués of Little Holland House said of Julia, who carelessly draped herself with lace and Indian shawls, that 'to all that knew her she remains a unique figure, baffling all description. . . . She doubled the generosity of the most generous of the sisters, and the impulsiveness of the most impulsive. If they were enthusiastic, she was so twice over; if they were persuasive, she was invincible. . . . If she had little of the beauty of her sisters, she certainly had remarkably fine eyes, that flashed like her sayings, or grew soft and tender if she was moved. . . . Like her eyes, her wit flashed out also.'[8] Although plainer than her sisters, when Watts painted her he carefully softened her features. He produced an attractive portrait of 'a woman of noble plainness carrying herself with dignity and expression, and well able to set off the laces and Indian shawls she wore so carelessly'.[9]

The painter, Spencer Stanhope, believed the secret that made Little Holland House so delightful was that there were no books there and everybody had to make an effort to talk. Leslie Stephen, who went to Little Holland House quite often (he was to be the second husband of Julia, daughter of Maria Jackson) said it was far less alarming there than at the Leweses', where you had to be ready to discuss metaphysics or the principles of aesthetic philosophy and be prepared to worship George Eliot. Thoby Prinsep sat at the edge of this social whirlpool, left the organising to his wife, smiled benignly at visitors and went for walks in the garden or composed Indian stories in verse.

Favoured guests were asked to stay on to dinner and the emancipated character and atmosphere of these gatherings was a far cry from the conventional stultified

Sundays of the early Victorian era. No doubt for that reason they attracted some waspish remarks. Writing of them, George du Maurier remarked on the 'slight element of looseness' at Little Holland House, called the Prinseps cultural snobs and said that tea was handed out to a bevy of Pre-Raphaelites by Mrs Prinsep and her sisters 'almost kneeling'. Lady Charlotte Schreiber, the diarist, commented that there couldn't be a worse place to go alone than Little Holland House, with musicians and artists talking 'flattery and nonsense', while a friend of Lord Holland's called it a hornets' nest.

Some of these remarks justified Julia's previously scathing remarks about Sarah's socialising. Nevertheless, Julia benefited enormously from meeting this circle of people. When, some ten years or so later, she became a professional photographer, she drew on almost all of them for subjects.

FOUR

'WIDE-BEAMING BENEVOLENCE'

While the Prinseps stayed in Little Holland House for twenty-three years, the Camerons moved around much more frequently. Although Charles was fifty-three years old when they returned to England, a respected age for those days, Julia at thirty-three was still full of drive. After they arrived in 1848, they first went to live at Ephraim Common at Tunbridge Wells in Kent, where they stayed less than two years. By then, three of their five sons were at school while the two youngest were at home with them, along with their daughter. Their neighbour in Kent was Henry Taylor, a Colonial Office administrator and the much praised author of the poetic drama, *Philip van Artevelde*, which had made his name. Charles Cameron had known him since they were both young men. Julia was delighted to meet him, agreeing with the critics who thought his drama a work of genius. As Tennyson's grandson was to say, 'Mrs Cameron was a woman of volcanic energy, with a romantic passion for the arts and an immense capacity for hero-worship.'[1] She immediately adopted the Taylors as her close friends: indeed, Taylor was referred to in the Camerons' house as 'Philip', after the title of his drama.

Goethe once claimed that all men and women were either natural anvils or hammers. Julia qualified as a hammer and Taylor considered she had 'a power of loving' which he had never seen exceeded, along with 'an equal determination to be beloved'. Julia was an intensely loyal friend. William Allingham, the Irish poet and diarist, remembered once sharing a carriage with her, when she told him she had a copy of Henry Taylor's works for him as a Christmas box. She then examined him as to his opinion of Taylor's poetry. It became clear that Allingham was not an admirer, and as a result the Christmas box was withheld and never mentioned again. She was bolstered by a letter from Richard Doyle saying he found Taylor's works were characterised by 'a serene and lofty grace', as well as by a letter from Sir John Herschel saying he was glad to learn that he and Julia's husband coincided entirely on the merits of Taylor as a poet.

Past friendships were not forgotten. Lord Hardinge wrote to Julia on 13 February 1850 about a memorial to another of her very dear friends, Major Broadfoot, telling her that he had arranged to see an artist 'who has designed a beautiful tablet as a tribute to dear Broadfoot's memory', and asking if he should call for her.[2]

Being generous to a fault, Julia overwhelmed her neighbours, the Taylors, with a positive cascade of presents which included, according to Taylor's rather exasperated account, 'her barbaric pearls and gold, Indian shawls, turquoise bracelets, inlaid portfolios, ivory elephants'. Taylor commented that 'The transference of her personal effects is going on day after day, and I think that shortly Cameron will find himself left with nothing but his real property.'[3] One Indian shawl that Julia gave his wife Alice was so costly that she felt she had to return it, with a tactful letter. Some time later Alice happened to pay a visit to the Putney Home for Incurables and was astonished to find an expensive sofa, designed to assist certain patients, had her name inscribed on it as donor. Julia had bought and paid for it by the sale of the shawl.

Julia was a tenacious, almost claustrophobically intense friend and when the Taylors decided to move from Tunbridge Wells to Leyden House, on the Thames at Mortlake, she unhesitatingly persuaded her husband that they must leave Tunbridge Wells immediately and find accommodation near to their friends. They looked around and were lucky enough to find a place that was nearby – Percy Lodge in Christchurch Road, East Sheen. Luckily the Taylors were delighted that the Camerons would remain their close neighbours.

Indeed, it says much for their friendship that it survived after Julia decided to surprise the Taylors by secretly working all night long in one of their bedrooms, repainting it in garish patterns (a currently fashionable craze) and showing them with delight the next morning how cleverly she had covered up their chosen original, elegant, light-coloured wood decor.

However, Alice Taylor was forgiving and wrote to her relations in 1850 to say that she was glad the Camerons had come to live nearby, saying of Julia, 'I have quite made up my mind about her and like her very much. She is a fine, generous creature, with many virtues and talent; but her great gift is that of loving others and forgetting herself.'[4] Julia had, Alice admitted, greatly increased their happiness because she was 'so full of loving sympathy for all our troubles and joys, great and small, and so full of resources and helpfulness in any case in which one wants help. She said she would make me love her as a sister, and I shook my head; but indeed she has won for herself the place she so much coveted of being the first of my friends and I sometimes wonder how I got on at all without her.'[5]

Julia met Alfred and Emily Tennyson for the first time at the Taylors' new Mortlake house on 21 October 1850 and was to form an equally intense friendship with them. Emily recorded her first sight of Mrs Cameron in her journal: 'That day she was a delightful picture in her dark green silk with wide open sleeves, the dress fastened by a silk cord round the waist and having the courtly charm of manner which was one of her many phases & one which became her right well.'[6] That year was an outstanding one for Tennyson. He published *In Memoriam*, which sold some 60,000 copies by the end of the year, was appointed Poet Laureate in succession to Wordsworth, and married Emily Sellwood.

Tennyson himself never really took to Henry Taylor – possibly because Taylor had always been rather patronising to him and they had been rivals for the laureateship after Wordsworth's death. Once, bored by Julia's constant over-the-top praise of Taylor, Tennyson pointed out that he did not see what she meant about his extraordinary beauty, as he considered he had a smile like a fish. Julia promptly replied, 'Only when the Spirit of the Lord moved on the face of the waters, Alfred.'[7] In later years, the two men became closer. Julia wrote to Taylor, in her usual forthright way, to tell him this: 'He [Tennyson] says he feels now he is beginning to know you, and not to feel afraid of you; and that he is beginning to get over your extreme insolence to him when he was young and you were in your meridian splendour.'[8]

In June 1852 Emily wrote the first of many letters to Julia to thank her for the happy day they had spent together at Kew Gardens. The Tennysons, who had been staying with various friends around England at the time, were looking for a place to buy, but Emily – who was expecting a baby in two months' time – assured Julia she was not going to drag her house-hunting 'even on paper'. Tennyson followed Taylor's recommendation that he should go and see the ivy-clad Chapel House, one of a fine row of early eighteenth-century houses in Montpelier Row, Twickenham. It was spacious, had fine views of the river, and Tennyson and his wife moved in.

Julia was particularly kind and helpful to Emily when the baby arrived unexpectedly soon, rushing to London to find a doctor, and returning with him to the Tennyson house to see what she too could do to help. Tennyson referred to Julia's 'wide beaming benevolence' and wrote to her saying he would never, to the hour of his death, forget her kindness. The friendship between them was cemented. When the couple's second baby was due in 1854 (he was to be called Hallam), Julia wrote to Tennyson for news: 'Day after day I get more anxious to hear . . . to know if I can be of any help or comfort.'

The letter was pages and pages long, mostly explaining why she hadn't written before. Julia had a passion for letter writing. Anne Thackeray remembered her sitting at her desk until the last moment of dispatch. 'Then, when the postman had hurried off, she would send the gardener running after him with some extra packet labelled "immediate". Soon after, the gardener's boy would follow pursuing the gardener with an important postscript, and, finally, I can remember the donkey being harnessed and driven galloping . . . arriving as the post-bags were being closed.'[9]

Although not quite such a ruthless big-name hunter as Sarah, Julia was still intensely socially ambitious. She adored the parties at Little Holland House and determined to set up her own literary and artistic circle at her East Sheen house, rivalling that at Little Holland House. Julia may not have had an in-house celebrity like Watts to wheel out, but she regarded Henry Taylor in the same light. Although today Taylor has fallen into obscurity, in the mid-nineteenth century he was very well known and respected. As well as *Philip van Artefelde*, his remarkable study in character, he wrote other tragedies, romantic comedies and lyrical poetry.

Thackeray, an old family friend, was a welcome guest at East Sheen. On one occasion, he took his two daughters, Anny and Minny, to visit Julia there. Anne Thackeray (Anny), was later to write: 'My father, who had known her [Julia] first as a girl in Paris, laughed and said: "She is quite unchanged . . . generous, unconventional, loyal and unexpected."'[10]

Julia was certainly unconventional — all the sisters were — but she was more determined than most, at times being positively hectoring in her resolve to get her own way. This particularly struck Anne during this same visit. She was impressed by Julia's dynamic energy, hypnotic personality and iron will 'which compelled everyone whether they liked it or not to do her bidding and carry out her most extravagant whims and fancies'.

Anne had been rather startled by her first sight of Julia: 'I remember a strange apparition in a flowing red velvet dress, although it was summer time, cordially welcoming us to a fine house and some belated meal when the attendant butler was addressed by her as 'man' and was ordered to do many things for our benefit; to bring back the luncheon dishes and curries for which Mrs Cameron and her family had a speciality.' When they left, Julia accompanied them to the station, bareheaded and trailing her draperies. Another friend told them she had accompanied him in the same way, only that time she carried a cup of tea with her which she stirred as she walked along.[11]

Anne recalled a further meeting with Julia in London when they went together to a chapel to hear a preacher called Brookfield. Julia sat down firmly in front of the pulpit and when Brookfield climbed the pulpit stairs to give his sermon, he was so near the women could easily have touched him. Julia promptly and repeatedly kissed her hand to him, which so deeply embarrassed him that he suddenly sank down on his knees and buried his head in the pulpit cushion.

Another old friend was Sir John Herschel, the celebrated astronomer – who first saw the great comet of 1857 in the grounds of Little Holland House. Writing of him Julia said, 'He was to me as a Teacher and High Priest. From my earliest girlhood I had loved and honoured him. . . . I was then residing in Calcutta, and scientific discoveries sent to that then benighted land were water to the parched lips of the starved.'[12] Their friendship was renewed when the Camerons returned to England. Julia was already godmother to one of Herschel's children and he in turn became godfather to her youngest son. The ceremony took place at Mortlake church and the other two godparents were Henry Taylor and Julia's sister, Virginia.

Her newer acquaintances were growing quickly through meeting the many friends of the Taylors and the Tennysons. The diarist Lady Charlotte Schreiber remembered an evening in 1856 when Dante Gabriel Rossetti and Holman Hunt were there (perhaps syphoned from Sarah) and Edward Lear entertained them by singing some of Tennyson's poems which he had set to music. Julia, in her element, very often declaimed the poetry of guests like Tennyson. That same year, the Tennysons, who had been looking around for several years at various properties, made their final payment on their new house, Farringford, on the Isle of Wight.

Julia herself made inroads into the literary world. Her translation of the long German narrative poem *Leonora*, by Gottfried August Burger, illustrated by Daniel Maclise, had been published back in 1847. She also wrote poetry, including some verses after the death of the poet Arthur Clough and a poem for *Macmillan's Magazine* in 1876. She produced a fragment of autobiography, *Annals of My Glasshouse*.

The Camerons now decided to leave their house at East Sheen and move once more, this time to Ashburton Cottage on Putney Heath, not far from their previous house. They stayed there several years. By now their older sons had finished their schooling, leaving just the two younger ones to be looked after at home. Julia had a close relationship with her own sons, was very fond of children generally and was always devastated if anything happened to the children of those she loved. It was from Ashburton Cottage, on 5 April 1859, that she wrote to Henry Halford Vaughan, husband of the eldest daughter of her sister, Maria Jackson. It was a heart-rendingly sympathetic letter, commiserating with him on the death of their only son. More happily, the Camerons' daughter Julia, who had come out by then, became engaged to a Charles Norman and married him that year.

Julia remained as busy as ever, writing to friends as well as seeing them. She was forty-four years old now, but still full of bustling energy. Watts, who had nearly completed a fresco at Lincoln's Inn on which he had been working for some time, and had allowed some friends to see it, wrote to Henry Taylor in the September of that year, thanking him for his comments. He added, 'Mrs Cameron's enthusiastic and extravagant admiration is really painful to me, for I feel as if I were practising a deception upon her. She describes a great picture, but it is hers and not mine . . . my pride is more hurt by over-estimation than by want of appreciation. . . .'[13]

It was at the end of 1859 that Charles Cameron decided to leave for another trip to Ceylon. He had recently heard the worrying news that his coffee crop in the Dimbula and Dikoya valleys had failed and he wanted to go and see the situation for himself. With him he took his eldest son, who was to stay out there and work, returning occasionally 'to gladden his mother's warm breast, to add up her bills, to admonish her, to cheer and enliven the house'.

Julia hated the thought of the two of them going away, and had previously become ill and distressed when her husband left on trips for any length of time. She wrote to Emily Tennyson to say she was drowned in troubles and cares and dismayed at seeing the portmanteaux being dragged out. She was almost glad when Charles was delayed by a bout of illness and went into overdrive to look after him. Any doctor she hadn't brought in herself was invariably accused of culpable carelessness or profound ignorance, but Charles might well have preferred their ministrations to Julia's own prescription which was ten drops of Jeremie's opiate every morning, a dose of creosote, zinc and gum arabic before meals, and a dose of quinine afterwards.

However, her kindness always shone through her over-forceful, managing behaviour. As Anne Thackeray said, 'She played the game of life with such vivid courage and disregard for ordinary rules; she entered into other people's interests with such warm hearted sympathy and determined devotion that, though her subjects may have occasionally rebelled, they generally ended by gratefully succumbing to her rule, laughing and protesting all the time.'[14]

Having regained his strength, Charles was still anxious to leave England (and his medicine), believing the sea voyage and the warmth of Ceylon would help him finally recuperate. In November 1859 he left, wrote Julia, for 'his wild woods & favourite forests & seductive Estates of Ceylon & he has taken my two eldest boys Eugene & Ewen with him'.[15] She would liked to have accompanied him but she had her younger sons to look after, and her daughter Julia, now aged twenty, was expecting her first child – an event she disgustedly thought should have convinced her husband to stay in England. 'Charles speaks to me of the flower of the coffee plant. I tell him that the eyes of the first grandchild should be more beautiful than any flower.'[16] As her husband said of the sisters, they are 'like tigers where their offspring are concerned'.

To take her mind off the parting, Alfred Tennyson, who had gone to see the Camerons off, took her back to stay with his family on the Isle of Wight. The Isle was considered so remote at that time that one of the porters at Yarmouth would call out to travellers waiting to get the steamer to Lymington on the mainland, 'This way for England'. To get from Yarmouth to Freshwater, where the Tennysons lived, one had to go by coach and horses.

While Julia was staying there, she made an impulsive decision to move the family to the island – though still holding on to the Putney Heath house. Charles had, in fact, already been to the island several times, visiting Tennyson, and Julia knew how much he liked it. She bought two adjoining houses on the roadside, with bay windows and low picturesque gables, that stood midway between the Tennysons' house, Farringford, and the cliffs, rocks and sea at Freshwater Bay. They could cut through country lanes and downs to the Tennysons' house in five minutes. Indeed, Julia built a special gate in the garden wall at the back to allow Tennyson to walk there through the fields from his house and avoid the dozens of trippers waiting to see England's popular poet.

Julia later had the two houses made into one by means of a linking tower in the centre. However, she kept them separate until 1871, deciding the family could live in the one nearer to the road and leave the other for her guests. The whole house was an attractive sight. One visitor remembers the walls being covered in ivy, passion flower and luxuriant Virginia creeper, which covered up the bare spaces in the front and wreathed the window frames.

Julia called the house 'Dimbola' to please Charles, after one of the coffee estates he was currently visiting in Ceylon. At forty-four, a new chapter of her life was about to begin.

FIVE

DIMBOLA LODGE

Back in Putney Heath, letters flew between Julia and Emily Tennyson as there was so much to arrange about the new house. The Tennysons helped with the negotiations to insure the land with business agents, purchases and furnishings. They also sent in their gardener to landscape the grounds and plant a hedge of black bay and copper beech. Julia, adrenalin to the fore, ran to and fro from Putney to Freshwater. In a note in her diary in April 1860, Emily wrote, 'Mrs Cameron coming from Town rushes in with a catalogue which she thinks will be helpful even before she has seen her children.'

Julia needed this preoccupation to distract her mind as she was missing her husband. Having been left almost alone for the first time made her feel miserable. In May 1860, after she and their two younger sons Charlie and Henry, had moved to the Island, she wrote to Charles to say delightedly that 'This island might equal your own island [Ceylon] now for a richness of effects. The downs are covered with golden gorse and beneath them the blue hyacinth is so thickly spread that the valleys look as if "the sky were upbreaking thro' the earth". The sea on

one side is cool and tranquil . . . the hedges are green . . .
the trees too are luxuriant.'[1]

However, most of her twenty-page letter was taken
up with an account of Tennyson's depression and of her
own sadness, without Charles there. She wrote to one of
her friends to say, 'I found that when I was with you the
tears were too near my eyes to venture to read aloud
Charles's letters. I am in very truth very unhappy. I
assume vivacity of manner for my own sake as well as
for others.'[2] Julia's need for Charles was strong: she
missed not just his companionship, but his intellectual
stimulation.

She wrote to him constantly as she was to do to her
sons when they were working in Ceylon. So full of the
latest news were these letters that, when in London, 'she
would go on mail days to the General Post Office and
write there, crying out from time to time, "How much
longer?" to which an enthralled clerk would reply, "Ten
minutes more" – "five" and so on, until the last second of
time to be allowed had come, when her letter was shut
and flung to the officials now waiting to seal up the last
sack.'[3] She once told her daughter, Julia, that in the last
fortnight she had written ninety-nine letters.

Charles accepted the move to the Isle of Wight – he
had no other option – and on his return wrote some
verses to his friends ('With little Yarmouth for my
nearest town'), apologising for leaving them, and
London.[4] Henry Taylor claimed Charles was not

particularly fond of the new house, but was quite content to see it full of guests. If he wanted seclusion, he went to bed.

The two young Cameron boys were much the same age as the Tennysons' two sons, Hallam and Lionel, and this was one of the reasons Julia was pleased at the move. She told Emily, 'how dear it will be for our children to grow and live happily together playing mad pranks along the healthy lea'.[5] Emily wasn't too sure about the pranks.

Dimbola filled Julia's time as she never stopped organising some new project or other. There were charades and picnics, walks by the sea and dinner parties. She helped coach the young people in plays for their amateur dramatics, which took place in a little theatre erected in the grounds. Anne Thackeray recalled her as being omnipresent, 'summoning one person and another, ordering all the day and long into the night, for of an evening came impromptu plays . . . and young partners dancing under the stars'.[6] She also had a special cottage built for Benjamin Jowett, Professor of Greek at Balliol College, Oxford, in order that he could bring his students there during the long vacation. He said that she had a tendency to make the house shake as soon as she entered it.

One visitor said that Dimbola soon acquired the character of 'Little Holland House-on-Sea'. Wilfred Ward, son of William Ward, the theologian and author of

The Ideal of a Christian Church, who lived nearby and was
a frequent visitor, was much impressed and wrote, 'The
Freshwater Society of which Tennyson was the centre in
the 'sixties and 'seventies approached, I think, nearer to
realizing the purpose and ideal of a French salon than
any social group I have myself known in England.' He
thought that this was mainly due to Julia's keen, eager
spirit which naturally created incident and interest.[7]

The Taylors, who took a house at Bournemouth each
summer, usually came to visit Julia at Dimbola every
spring and autumn, staying a fortnight at a time.
Sometimes his wife, busy unpacking at the house, sent
Henry off on his own. He was quite happy, aware that all
men, women and children were welcome and had a very
pleasurable time there, liking its unconventionality and
saying with amusement that it reminded him of the way
one old English aristocrat received guests with the
peremptory comment that his house was Liberty Hall
but 'if everybody doesn't do as he likes here, by God, I'll
make him'.

Visiting the Camerons in April 1861, he went up to
the schoolroom to see the boys and noticed an
exceedingly attractive girl of thirteen called Mary Ryan
sharing their lessons. He thought her a friend, but it
turned out she and her mother were Irish beggars who
had accosted Julia on Putney Heath. Struck by the
child's beauty, she had taken them both home, given the
mother work and proceeded to bring the child up with

her own boys. Henry Taylor wondered whatever would become of her, but Julia decided to let time take care of that. Mary eventually became Julia's parlourmaid, photographic assistant and model. And in true story-book fashion, she met a wealthy young man, Henry Cotton (later Sir Henry Cotton), who had dropped in to see an exhibition of Julia's photographs of her. He was struck by these and by the beauty of Mary, who was there at the time. They married and lived happily ever after.

On that same visit, Julia was concerned that the room that Taylor was to occupy was too dark and decided to install a west-facing window. She called in a builder and carpenter to work through the night, summoned a glazier the next day, and by the time Henry Taylor arrived a maid was putting the final stitches into the muslin curtain.

Julia was forty-six years old and at times behaved like a hectic teenager. Her sudden, quirky decisions like this were legendary. Once, finding a complete stranger had lost his hat in a strong wind, she took him home so that he could choose one of her husband's hats to wear instead. And once, introducing some guests to Henry Taylor one lunchtime, she was forced to ask their names as she had spontaneously asked them to lunch when they had met the day before on the steamboat. On another occasion, knowing her husband felt the vegetable garden took up too much space and preferred lawn, and not wishing to disturb his daily walks in the garden, Julia gave orders for the transition to be carried out in total secrecy one night. Turf was therefore brought in cartloads and, under the light of lanterns, the vegetable garden was swept away. The next morning, looking out of the window, Charles was astonished to see a perfect green lawn had replaced the vegetable garden. From then on he was to be seen pacing up and down it, spouting Homer or Theocritus to one of his boys. Tennyson admired Charles's erudition and respected Julia's opinion. Agnes Weld, Emily Tennyson's niece, recalls that Tennyson would bring his new poems and plays down to Dimbola Lodge and read them aloud to the Camerons, while their sons sat in reverential silence on the floor.

Julia never counted the cost of her quirky extravagances. Her husband, aware of the dwindling resources from his coffee estates, would shake his head and say to friends, 'Julia is carving up Ceylon.' He realised with affectionate amusement that she was unstoppable. As Anne Thackeray said, 'No words could describe Mrs Cameron, her dynamic energy, her hypnotic personality, and her iron will, which compelled everyone whether they liked it or not to do her bidding and carry out her most extravagant whims and fancies.'[8] Henry Taylor's wife Alice, felt this too. Despite Julia being an old friend, she wrote to her husband to say that the two of them had visited Professor Benjamin Jowett and that she had felt very shy 'as I always do when I am in society with Mrs. Cameron. She steers; and so oddly and so boldly that I always expect to find myself stuck in a quicksand or broken against a rock.'[9]

With Julia, interference was an art form. Anne Thackeray, among others, did not stand in her way. She realised that Julia was a masterful woman, 'a friend with enough of the foe in her generous composition to make any of us hesitate who ventured to cross her decree'. Tennyson endured more from her than he would from anyone else. She turned up at his house at all hours, convenient and inconvenient, entering by the door, the drawing-room window, bringing goodwill and life with her. 'She would walk in at night followed by friends, by sons carrying lanterns, by nieces, by maids bearing parcels and photographs.'[10] Edward Lear, who was staying with the Tennysons in June 1860, was taken aback at seeing Julia sweep into Farringford one evening, followed by eight men tramping up the drive carrying a grand piano – a better instrument than the Tennysons' own 'polykettlejarring' one – so that he would be able to play and sing for them. Lear was immediately angry that such 'odious incense, palaver & fuss succeeded the quiet home moments'.

Lear might not have been amused, but Julia was thoroughly enjoying social life. At one dinner party with the Tennysons, she wrote of how they had sat down at seven o'clock and only got up from the table at eleven.

Julia Margaret Cameron and her youngest sons, Henry Herschel Hay and
Charles Hay, by Lewis Carroll, *c.* 1860.
(*Wilson Centre for Photography*)

The actress Ellen Terry, just after her seventeenth birthday in 1864, when she and her husband, G.F. Watts, shortly after their marriage, went to stay with the Camerons on the Isle of Wight. This remarkable photograph shows Terry as half-child, half-woman. (*Royal Photographic Society*)

Sir Henry Taylor, author of the then acclaimed poetic drama *Philip van Artefelde*, 1864. He was both mentor and long-standing friend, and Cameron praised him for unselfishly modelling for her. (*Wilson Centre for Photography*)

Paul and Virginia, *c.* 1865. The young sitters were Freddy Gould and Lizzie Keown. This was based on *Paul et Virginie*, a romance by Bernardin de Saint Pierre which, though written in 1795, was highly popular with Victorians. (*Wilson Centre for Photography*)

'Whisper of the Muse' was taken in 1865 with G.F. Watts (not known for any musical ability) as centre figure, holding the fiddle. (*Wilson Centre for Photography*)

'Mountain Nymph Sweet Liberty', 1866. The title is from Milton's *L'Allegro*. Commenting on it, the astronomer Sir John Herschel said it was 'a most *astonishing* piece of high relief'. (*Wilson Centre for Photography*)

Cameron referred to Sir John Herschel as her 'Teacher and High Priest', and this 1867 portrait is regarded as one of her very finest. (*Wilson Centre for Photography*)

This portrait of Julia Margaret Cameron was taken by her son, Henry Herschel Hay Cameron, in 1870, when she was fifty-five. (*Wilson Centre for Photography*)

Charles Hay Cameron, 1871. 'My husband from first to last has watched every picture with delight' was his wife's comment. Their marriage was exceptionally happy. (*Wilson Centre for Photography*)

Mrs Herbert Duckworth, 1872. Mrs Duckworth, regarded as a beauty, was Cameron's niece, being the daughter of Julia's sister, Maria (Mia) Jackson. (*Wilson Centre for Photography*)

'The Parting of Sir Lancelot and Queen Guinevere', one of Cameron's most poignant illustrations to Tennyson's *Idylls of the King*. She selected her models for the Camelot saga carefully and only found a suitable Lancelot at the last minute. (*Wilson Centre for Photography*)

Alfred Tennyson was one of Cameron's greatest friends. They were neighbours on the Isle of Wight and this photograph, from 1875, is one of the many she took of him. (*Wilson Centre for Photography*)

'All the while the most brilliant conversation. The whole range of poetry, comprising every immortal poet brought to life and living again in the glowing wise breath of Alfred Tennyson and the quotations from Henry Taylor's rich and faithful memory – they were like two brilliant fencers crossing their rapiers.'[11]

Julia's fondness for the Tennysons resulted in her bestowing a range of gifts on them including two legs of Welsh mutton, some vivid blue paper with a border from the Elgin marbles ('the vivid blue neither she nor we like') and 'one of her lucky purchases of pictures', which the Tennysons sensibly refused.[12] Emily wrote, half laughing to her, 'The only drawback is the old complaint that you will rain down precious things upon us, not drop by drop but in whole Golconda mines at once.'[13] But it was impossible to snub Julia, as her friends recognised her essential kindness. She wrote, for instance, to the poet Arthur Clough in July 1862 to say the Tennysons had just left to stay at her 'dear little house' in Putney Heath and would be his near neighbours. Could her dearest Mr Clough, if he had the use of a carriage, 'take up Mrs Tennyson, and give her an opportunity of seeing people and things without the wear and tear of her delicate health?'[14]

Julia was one of the few people allowed to call Tennyson by his Christian name and he, in turn, called her Julia. Both intimidated other people: neither intimidated each other. Julia thought his entourage too serious and made no attempt to flatter him, possibly because she regarded Henry Taylor as the greater poet. Her bracing honesty and complete lack of ceremony was a welcome change for Tennyson. She unhesitatingly told him what she thought of his behaviour, ordered him around and he usually, resignedly gave in to her. Once during an outbreak of smallpox in the village, Julia discovered that Tennyson had refused to be vaccinated. She went straight to the doctor and asked him to accompany her to Farringford. Spotting them, Tennyson promptly bolted upstairs and locked himself in his study, whereupon Julia stood at the bottom of the stairs and shouted up at regular intervals, 'You're a coward, Alfred, a coward!' until Tennyson shouted back, 'Woman, go away, I will be vaccinated tomorrow.' He was, but unfortunately the vaccine was faulty and he took some time to recover from an inflamed leg and a fever.

Julia's kindness, over the years, however, lifted Emily's spirits, particularly when Alfred was away. She wrote in her journal that 'I should have been dreary as . . . I cannot see to read by candlelight, had not dear Mrs Cameron come to me night by night for an hour.' And on another occasion she recalled her pleasure at seeing Julia coming across the park, 'looking gorgeous in her violet dress and red cloak, walking over the newly mown grass. Pleasant to hear the men cheering.'[15] Tennyson, who went to London with Julia in the summer of 1863, commented more acidly on Julia's habit of bribing the guard so that she got a carriage on her own. She continued to distribute her kindness around like confetti. Thackeray died that December and Julia promptly offered his daughters Anny and Minny part of Dimbola Lodge. Anny said that she was goodness in person.

Effervescent and vital and always the centre of a group, Julia was in stark contrast to her husband Charles, who once said that 'solitude has never been oppressive to me, nor is it so even now when I cannot occupy myself for any long time reading'.[16] A handsome man, with long white locks – Tennyson called him 'a philosopher with his beard dipped in moonlight' – he would sit at the head of the table, saying very little. On one occasion at a dinner party at Dimbola, he suddenly roused himself on hearing the word 'spirit' being mentioned by chance by a guest and pronounced ghoulishly, 'I shall soon be a spirit.' After dinner was over and everyone had moved into an adjacent room, Charles remained where he was and Julia fondly wrapped him up in a shawl, leaving very little of him to be seen. He stayed there looking 'like a piece of furniture in an untenanted house'. Another time, Julia took a guest up to his bedroom where he lay fast asleep and told her, dramatically, to behold the most beautiful old man on earth. The guest asked who he was, and Julia replied proudly that it was her husband.

In 1863, Charles went out to Ceylon again as the news from the coffee estates there was still worrying.

He was also interested in applying for the Governorship. Henry Taylor was asked by the Secretary of State whether he thought this post should be offered to him, but the final conclusion was that Charles's health was unequal to it. Julia again desperately missed her husband and her two sons, Ewen and Charles, who were working out there. She was very conscious that the family circle was shrinking now that her sons were busy leading their own lives: Eugene was in the Royal Artillery and Hardinge was up at Oxford. Her volatile nature again plunged her into depression. To cheer her up, and alleviate her loneliness, her daughter Julia and her son-in-law Charles Norman invited her to stay. But even being with them could not prevent her deepening moods of depression. When she was leaving, her daughter was anxious to try and give her thoughts a new direction. She remembered the current craze for photography and in December of that year she gave Julia a camera with the words, 'It may amuse you, Mother, to try to photograph during your solitude at Freshwater.'

The remark has daughterly overtones of 'there-there-mother-keep-busy-and-you'll-soon-feel-better'. If Julia's daughter thought it would merely divert her mother's mind while her husband was away, she underestimated her – as a great many others were to do in the future. Admittedly, most Victorian women recipients would have amused themselves with such a complicated gift for a month or so and then put it quietly away in a cupboard. But Julia was not interested in dabbling: she was in need of a challenge. Photography for her was to become a passion: she was a woman with exceptional vitality and determination and now she added ambition to these qualities.

Until now she had always expended her whirlwind energy on her friends, but rather like a sparkling Catherine wheel this energy went round and round but had no real place to go. From now on she harnessed it to one end, that of taking some of the most spectacular photographs of the age.

THROUGH THE
LOOKING-GLASS

Julia was forty-eight years old when she received the gift of her first camera. The one she was given, along with the necessary darkroom outfit, was cumbersome — as indeed they all were in those days. It was basically two large wooden boxes, one sliding within the other by a rack and pinion movement, which took plates of 9 × 11 inches. A French 'Jamin' lens went with it, which had a focal length of 12 in.

Writing autobiographically in *Annals of My Glasshouse*, she said that the gift of a camera 'from those I loved so tenderly added more and more impulse to my deeply-seated love for the beautiful, and from the first moment I handled my lens with a tender ardour, it has become to me as a living thing, with voice and memory and creative vigour.' She may have handled her lens with a tender ardour, but she also displayed, from the start, a ruthless perfectionism. The quality and power of her best photographs were due to her rigorous standards. She stated that her aims, from the start, were high. They were, 'to ennoble Photography and to secure for it the

character and uses of High Art by combining the real &
ideal sacrificing nothing of Truth by all possible devotion
to Poetry & Beauty'.

At the time, the stiff portraiture of the mid-Victorian
era filled the albums of every middle-class family.
Photographs were chiefly regarded as a documentary, a
way of recording faces and families. Husbands, wives
and children sat or stood without expression, stiffly,
hand on the antimacassar; whiskered men leant on
broken pillars; crinolined women peered into mirrors
which reflected their own faces. Nevertheless,
photography had become a craze. Albums bulged with
photos of people or places; penny-in-the-slot photos of
celebrities were collected by the score and small carte-
de-visite portraits, on thick cards, were constantly
exchanged between friends. Despite their universally
wooden look they were immensely popular: one firm
alone claimed to sell more than 50,000 of these a
month.

Julia's extraordinary photographs broke the mould
with a vengeance: she used imagination, creating an
artistic work. Her different vision of photography from
the usual rigid poses, developed from her conviction
that photography was an art, like painting. She said, 'I
longed to arrest all beauty that came before me.' The
camera, to her, was a way of creating beauty. She showed
that it could create an art of its own and tried, in her
photography, to do what many artists were doing in

paint. Many of her ideas for subjects came from paintings.

During her first year of taking photographs Julia said that she worked fruitlessly but not hopelessly. She overcame obstacles which could well have defeated anyone less determined. Her great-niece, Laura Troubridge, recalled that Julia was totally absorbed by her photography and behaved indeed 'like one possessed, a tyrant to herself and her sitters'. To Laura, as a child, Julia appeared 'as a terrifying elderly woman, short and squat, with none of the Pattle grace and beauty about her, though more than her share of their passionate energy and wilfulness. Dressed in dark clothes, stained with chemicals from her photography (and smelling of them, too) with a plump, eager face and piercing eyes and a voice husky, and a little harsh, yet in some way compelling and even charming.'[1]

The first photograph Julia took was that of a farmer at Freshwater. It took her hours of experiment until she succeeded in getting a good image and proved very expensive as she was paying him 2s 6d an hour. This was the photograph she then inadvertently spoiled by smudging it before it dried. Right from the beginning she was not interested merely in imprinting an image on paper. She chose this particular farmer because it seemed to her that he resembled Bolingbroke. Already her vision of the way she saw her subjects and what she wanted to photograph was emerging.

She once broke off a conversation with a friend and rushed off at full speed after a passing old man, with white hair, who happened to be holding a scythe, calling out 'Stop him, stop him; there goes Time.' Emily Tennyson, writing to her father, said 'According to Hallam [her eldest son] he was undressed, had no shirt on. Wanted scrubbing very much. Mrs Cameron wraps him up in best shawls, puts an egg cup in his hand, turns him into "Time", but talks to him so much about his beautiful face that he is supposed to have grown very conceited at last.'[2] On another occasion, Julia saw her ideal of an ancient Egyptian walking down some steps into an Oxford kitchen. She called on the young woman's mistress, a complete stranger, and persuaded her to part with her cook for several days. Julia then took 'a truly magnificent photograph of this superb reincarnation of the Greco-Egyptian type'.

Julia's second subject was two children. However, one of these started to splutter with laughter halfway through the process, and by moving spoilt the picture. Julia decided it was simpler to concentrate on one child alone and took her aside to beg her not to move as if she did she would 'waste poor Mrs Cameron's chemicals and strength'.

The child rewarded her by remaining still and the resulting photograph thrilled and inspired Julia, who called it her first success. 'I was in a transport of delight. I ran all over the house to search for gifts for the child. I felt as if she entirely had made the picture. I printed, toned, fixed and framed it, and presented it to her father that same day: size 11 by 9 inches.'[3] The date on the photograph was January 1864.

Her most highly praised works were her portraits of 'Famous Men and Fair Women'. Writing to Sir John Herschel about them, she said, 'I have just been *engaged* in doing that which Mr Watts has long been urging me to do – a series of Life sized heads – They are not only *From* the Life but *to* the Life and startle the eye with wonder & delight. I hope they will astound the Public & *reveal* more of the mystery of this heaven & our art – They lose nothing in beauty & gain much in power.'[4] They were certainly powerful enough to astound the Victorian public.

Julia virtually invented the art of the portrait photograph. Laura Troubridge said that 'No one had ever undertaken a real portrait study until Aunt Julia, with her hobby and her unconventionality, revolutionised all previous ideas upon the subject by producing, though in a rough and unfinished state, what were in reality works of art.'[5] Colin Ford, the Cameron scholar, in his book *The Cameron Collection*, stresses that 'The strength in Mrs Cameron's portraits comes from the power of the faces she chose to photograph; the intensity of their gaze is increased by their having had to sit motionless before the unblinking eye of her camera for minutes at a time.'[6]

Julia agreed with Watts that a portrait must be 'the window of the soul' and many of her portraits of the famous perceptively illuminated their inner spirit. The length of time her exposures took (three to seven minutes), the sense of occasion, the concentration required – all contributed to the sitters revealing some essence of themselves. She achieved her effect by the then revolutionary use of close-ups and by dramatic lighting. Most photographers of the time had large windows and skylights in their studios and they used as much light as they could as this cut down the exposure time to thirty seconds or so. Their photographs came out brightly lit – and one-dimensional. Julia on the other hand was constantly experimenting with the effects of light, cutting out the light from the windows, using dark backgrounds and sometimes a black velvet cloth as drapery. The results were intimate and penetrating.

She had a gift for knowing how to achieve what she wanted. When she was photographing Sir John Herschel, she got him to wash his hair first which made it stand out in a halo around his head. This focused attention on his face, giving it an intensity of expression.

Much of this was instinct – and she always followed her instinct, ignoring criticism or ridicule. She began without any identifiable technique or knowledge of photography and had to learn every painful step through trial and error. As she said, 'I did not know where to place my dark box, how to focus my sitter and my first picture I effaced to my consternation by rubbing my hand over the filmy side of the glass. . . . I turned my coal house into my dark room, and a glazed fowl-house I had given to my children became my glass house. The hens were liberated, I hope and believe not eaten.'[7] One sitter described her glass house as being very untidy and very uncomfortable. Inside, it was very simple. Unlike most portrait studios in Victorian England – which had as much heavy clutter in them as most Victorian houses – Julia offered just a chair and a dark curtain as backdrop. She worked there with three assistants, her maids Ellen Ottington, Kate Shepherd and Mary Hillier. Mary, who lived locally, was a most beautiful girl who sat for Julia a great many times and was in a large number of her Madonna studies – so much so that she became known as 'Mary Madonna' or 'The Island Madonna'.

Ignorant about photographic technique, Julia, at the start, was dependent for knowledge on the detailed and complicated articles that were currently being written about the different methods of photography and the ways these were evolving. She was able to call on her brother-in-law, Lord Somers, for advice as he was a dedicated amateur photographer, and on her friend, the Astronomer Royal, Sir John Herschel. She thanked him for the insight into photography he had given her and told him all her difficulties: 'All through this severe month of January [1864] I felt my way literally in the dark thro' endless failures.'[8] In their frequent exchange of letters, Herschel often gave her advice on chemicals. In one letter he warned her, almost frantically, about the dangers of letting 'that dreadful poison' the cyanide of potassium run all over her hands: 'Pray! Pray! Be more cautious.' He sent her a cutting from a photographic magazine about the way she could remove stains by the use of harmless chemicals.

The more harmful chemicals caused many a dramatic scene at Dimbola. One acquaintance, dropping in one morning, found Julia 'pacing up and down in the downstairs morning room with a son at each elbow, urging their mother to keep moving and all three in a state of great agitation. It appeared that she had got some poisonous photographic mixture into a cut and they were all persuaded that to sit down meant some sort of fatal drowsiness.'[9] The acquaintance went for the doctor, but all turned out well.

The developing process Julia used – that of collodion plates – had only been introduced in the last decade or so. Frederick Scott Archer, a sculptor, had been experimenting since 1848 with collodion, a tough, transparent colourless film (its name was derived from the Greek word for 'glue').

Archer published his findings in March 1851, disclosing that first he coated a spotlessly clean glass plate evenly with collodion (which one could buy ready-made). This meant holding the plate between thumb and fingers and tilting it so the collodion covered the whole surface. After the collodion had set, but before it dried, he dipped the plate in a bath of silver nitrate to sensitise it. He then took the plate out in semi-darkness, placed it in a slide, inserted it in the camera, and made the exposure. Each exposure lasted between three and five minutes. The plate had to be handled with extreme care to avoid making an indelible scratch or mark. It also had to be developed immediately while it was still wet from collodion (the standard developers used were either ferrous sulphate or potassium cyanide).

The developer, like the collodion, had to be poured very evenly over the plate. Archer then fixed it with sodium thiosulphate, and washed the plate in water. Next he dried it by warming it 'as hot as the back of the hand will bear' and finally poured varnish on it. This protected the coating, which was necessary before any proofs could be printed from it.[10]

It was absolutely crucial the plate was sensitised, exposed and processed while the collodion was still wet or the silver nitrate would crystallise as it dried. This would cause a net-like pattern which showed up on the print. It explains why the technique was popularly referred to as the 'wet plate' process. A glass plate was used rather than paper, as glass had no grain in it, so gave a better definition than a paper negative. But Julia printed her negatives on commercially prepared albumen (egg white) paper, which she sensitised with silver chloride. Silver chloride paper was thought to give photographs a better definition.

There was no running water in Julia's darkroom and she wrote to her Calcutta friend, Sir Edward Ryan, to say how much work this was causing her as even in freezing weather she had to pour nine cans of water straight from the well over each photograph. Anne Thackeray said that she 'paddles in cold water till two o'clock every morning'. Julia was not known for her delicacy of movement and painstaking approach: she was impetuous and even clumsy. Nevertheless, she had the patience to carry out this meticulous and complicated process, saying that the difficulty 'enhanced the value of the pursuit'. She would sometimes expose a large number of plates until she got the result she wanted.

Indeed Watts's second wife, Mary (whom he married in 1886), said Julia told her that she would destroy a hundred negatives before achieving one good result, 'her object being to overcome realism by diminishing just in the least degree the precision of the focus'. When she was successful, therefore, she could give to her work 'a poetry and a mystery far removed from the work of the ordinary photographer. While other photographs, after long acquaintance, weary the eye, hers remain always an abiding pleasure.'[11]

The entire, complicated and messy process of photography might, understandably, have made the average Victorian woman, presented with a camera, reel back and return to her sketchbook. And indeed women were expected – by most male photographers of the time – to regard photography as merely an amusing hobby. But Julia was fascinated by the whole process. She was ambitious and extremely confident in an art which itself was at an early stage. She wanted to push out the boundaries and it annoyed her to realise that any inexperienced person who chose to put up an easel and sit in front of a landscape was promptly dubbed 'an artist', whereas photographers were – just photographers.

She herself – intent on creating 'high art' – was certain that intelligence, beauty and spirituality were interrelated and aimed for this in her photographs. Her early ones were naturally still those of trial and error. But one of them, that of Ellen Terry leaning against some patterned wallpaper, a mixture of sensuality and innocence, is an extraordinarily beautiful study. Taken in 1864, nearly 140 years ago, it still shines out of the page, a luminous and exquisite example of girlhood verging on womanhood.

Ellen married G.F. Watts on 24 February 1864. It was three days after her seventeenth birthday and three days before his forty-seventh birthday. The marriage was condoned and practically initiated by Sarah Prinsep, who felt her 'Signor', as Watts was known at Little Holland House, needed company. The new couple had no formal honeymoon but shortly after their marriage, and chaperoned inevitably by Sarah and Thoby Prinsep, the two of them had gone to stay a few weeks with the Camerons at the Isle of Wight. Watts had long been friendly with them and the Tennysons: it was an ideal retreat.

Writing in her memoirs, Ellen said of the visit, 'I was still so young that I preferred playing Indians and Knights of the Round Table with Tennyson's sons, Hallam and Lionel, and the young Camerons, to sitting indoors noticing what the poet did and said . . . he and all the others seemed to me very old.' She loved the way Tennyson recited poetry in the evenings, thinking his reading of Browning's *How They Brought the Good News from Ghent to Aix*, making the words 'come out sharply like hoofs upon a road', better than anything of his own. She also thought that Tennyson looked like a poet, with his shock of dark hair and loose clothes, whereas Browning, with his smart coat and society manners, did not.[12]

Ellen's marriage to Watts ended within the year, much to her surprise and bewilderment. Sarah Prinsep, who had considerable influence over Watts, felt ultimately that Ellen was too young and feckless, too inadequate altogether, to make a good wife for him. In a letter to a friend of hers, Mary Ann Hall, in which she swore her to secrecy, Ellen said that 'Reports meet me on every side . . . of what Mr Watts has said of me – all most *cowardly* and *most untrue*. There is no shadow of doubt (for it has been *proved* to me) that *he* and not Mrs Prinsep only has said these things!! (I cd have forgiven the spite, and vexation of an *angry*, and *not* good woman).'[13]

It is not certain where in her house Julia photographed Ellen – it could even have been in Tennyson's house – but her husband Charles put up with the chaos she invariably created and was extremely encouraging and sympathetic about his wife's obsession with photography. She was the first to admit it and to acknowledge the importance of his support: 'My husband from first to last has watched every picture with delight, and it is my daily habit to run to him with every glass upon which a fresh glory is newly stamped, and to listen to his enthusiastic applause. This habit of running into the dining room with my wet pictures has stained such an immense quantity of table linen with nitrate of silver, indelible stains, that I should have been banished from any less indulgent household.'[14]

It has been argued that her portraits of men were far more impressive and dramatic than those she took of women and reinforced the myth of male dominance. This was because she frequently photographed men gazing directly at the camera, whereas with her female subjects she used softer lighting and a less searching approach. Violet Hamilton, in assessing her photographs in *Annals of My Glasshouse: Photographs by Julia Margaret*

Cameron, says that Julia 'created an ambiguity of expression which renders the mood of the subject elusive. Cameron achieved this effect in her photographs by varying the focus and depth of field.' She also makes the point that Julia 'selected a particular focus because it appealed to her aesthetic, which held that softened outlines were artistic'.[15]

Julia had a sympathetic eye for female beauty and though she photographed many women in profile, those she took full-face were quite as arresting and interesting as some of her male studies.

One striking full-face portrait of a woman who, far from passive, looks as forceful as a potential Lady Macbeth, is called 'Mountain Nymph Sweet Liberty' (after a passage in John Milton's *L'Allegro*). It was highly praised by Sir John Herschel who said the head, though 'a little *farouche* and *égarée*, by the way, as if first let loose and half afraid that it was too good' was 'really a most astonishing piece of high relief. She is absolutely alive and thrusting out her head from the paper into the air. This is your own special style.'[16] Sylvia Wolf in her book *Focus: Five Women Photographers* says that 'On the faces of Cameron's female subjects we read languor, melancholy, defiance and desire.'[17]

Another deliberately shadowed portrait of Julia's niece, Julia Jackson, again full-face, puts sharp focus on the eyes. One called 'Light Study', taken after sunset, shows the model staring ahead less dramatically, with the emphasis on the soft contours of her face in twilight. Ian Jeffrey comments in his book on photography that her work resembles that of Rembrandt: 'many of her figures emerge dramatically from darkness, with very little of dress or background in evidence'. To his eyes, they inhabit not the mundane world, but are projected into a spirit world of her own devising.[18]

The identity of the model for 'Mountain Nymph' is still uncertain. The photograph was taken in 1866, the year that the Camerons 'adopted' three children – Cyllena, Melita and Sheridan – orphans of their friend, the Revd Sheridan Wilson. Cyllena Wilson modelled for Julia several times over the years, and some say she posed for the 'Mountain Nymph'. Confusingly, however, her name appears under the images of other women. Cyllena was eventually to tire of constantly posing, particularly after one occasion when she had to represent 'Despair' and Julia decided she didn't look sad enough – so promptly locked her up in the cellar for two hours to enhance her expression. Unsurprisingly, Cyllena was to run away and take a job as stewardess on an Atlantic liner. Also in the 1860s the Camerons adopted the two orphaned granddaughters of Julia's elder sister Adeline (Mrs Colin Mackenzie), Mary and Adeline Clogstoun. This was in addition to Mary Ryan, who had been taken into the Cameron household in the 1850s and brought up with the rest of the family.

Aware that her photography was adding to the

household's spiralling costs, Julia was only too conscious of the need to make, rather than spend, money and tried hard to economise. Once she read an item about the recovery of silver from photographic solutions and rushed off to London with her solutions in bottles in an attempt to discover how to reclaim the metal. What she discovered instead, to her shock, was that she had spent more on the trip than the silver would have been worth. Unfortunately, her status as an amateur photographer meant that, unlike commercial photographers, she couldn't charge for taking photographs – though Tennyson tried on occasion to reimburse her for her materials. Darwin was the only sitter who once paid her.

Julia could have made money by being a jobbing photographer, but she had no wish to enter the commercial world. She was occasionally mistaken for one. She once received a letter from a Miss Lydia Louisa Summerhouse Donkins who informed her that she wished to sit for her photograph but that she was 'a carriage person' and could therefore 'assure Mrs Cameron that she would arrive with her dress uncrumpled'. Julia sent a brisk message back to say that not being a professional, she couldn't take her likeness – but had she been able to do so, she would prefer Miss Donkins's dress to be crumpled.[19]

Emily Tennyson, aware of Julia's need to make some money and conscious of the way she lavishly handed out her photographs to friends as gifts, tried to curb her generosity: 'I do not mean to let you ruin yourself by giving the photographs away. . . . I see that I shall have to set up a shop for the sale of photographs myself all for your benefit.'[20] But Julia's immense energy was channelled into photography rather than the sales side, and she never managed to be a commercial success.

SEVEN

'JULIA CAMERON, YOU ARE A DREADFUL WOMAN'

Julia's total commitment to her photographs resulted in her riding roughshod over her subjects, giving them an appalling time – though she was as unsparing of herself. She said after photographing W.G. Ward, a good friend of Tennyson, 'I counted four hundred and five hundred and got one good picture. Poor Wilfred said it was *torture* to sit long, that he was a martyr. I said that I am the martyr! Just try the taking instead of the sitting.'[1]

Her attitude became a joke, even if not appreciated by those involved. Virginia Woolf's affectionate, amusing send-up of Julia (her great-aunt) in her comedy play, *Freshwater*, begins with Julia washing her husband's hair before he posed, and saying to him, 'Sit still, Charles! Sit still! Soap in your eyes? Nonsense. Water down your back? Tush! Surely you can put up with a little discomfort in the cause of art!'[2]

There is a seemingly unending list of those who were put to far more discomfort. Anne Thackeray commented that sitting for her was a serious affair, not to be lightly entered upon. 'Her sitters came to her summons, they trembled, or would have trembled, could they have dared, when the round black eye of the Camera was turned upon them.'[3] They were made to realise the disastrous waste of time, money and effort that would result from one quiver of emotion. Julia intimidated practically every sitter she had – though wrapped up in her private world and intent only on her work, she was either unaware of this, or uncaring.

She once decided to photograph Laura Troubridge and her small friend as two of the angels of the Nativity, each scantily clad with a pair of heavy swan's wings fastened to their narrow shoulders. She tousled their hair to rid them of a nursery look. Laura said that she wasn't at all surprised that when she looked at the old photographs of her and her friend as angels, these showed them leaning wistfully and anxiously over the imaginary ramparts of heaven, as they never knew what 'Aunt Julia' was going to do next. They knew, however, that 'once in her clutches we were perfectly helpless'. She would shout at them to stand still, 'and we stood for hours, if necessary, gazing at the model of the Heavenly Babe' (in reality a sleeping child deposited in a makeshift manger). The parents, anxious and uneasy, were outside, 'no more able to rescue their infant until Aunt Julia had finished with it, than we should have been'.[4]

Freshwater in Tennyson's time has been lyrically (and exaggeratedly) likened to Athens in the time of Pericles: sooner or later, every famous man in Britain came to visit the poet. One visitor once asked, rather desperately, 'Is there *nobody* here who is commonplace?' Julia took advantage of the stream of Tennyson's guests, looking on them as potential subjects for her. In this way, she was to photograph practically every one of his eminent visitors. She didn't always succeed. On one occasion in the mid-sixties, when Garibaldi was staying with Tennyson, Julia, her hands blackened as usual with photographic chemicals, rushed up and knelt in front of the two men, imploring Garibaldi to come to the glasshouse at Dimbola and allow her to take his picture. 'For a moment there was a misunderstanding as Garibaldi took her for an overdressed beggar woman asking for charity. Mrs Cameron, realising what was passing through his mind, waved her hands in front of his face and explained, "This is not dirt but art!" Her plea failed.'[5] However, she did once manage to inveigle herself into the presence of the Crown Prince of Prussia when he and his wife came to Ventnor in strict secrecy, and managed to photograph him.

In general, however, Julia put the fear of God into all those who sat for her. Browning was left in a position of acute discomfort while Julia went off to find some missing equipment and only rescued him two hours later. She once thrust herself into Thomas Carlyle's bedroom while he was changing his trousers in order to discuss a suitable pose. On one occasion Tennyson brought Longfellow along to be photographed and left him with Julia, saying, 'Longfellow, you will have to do whatever she tells you. I will come back soon and see what is left of you.'[6]

Nevertheless, the results were usually applauded by the sitters. Carlyle said that though the photograph of him was 'terrifically ugly and woebegone' it did have a likeness. Darwin wrote under his photograph that he liked it better than any other.

One reason Tennyson tended to offer up his illustrious guests as sacrifice was in order to avoid Julia's constant requests to photograph him. She had indeed already done so very successfully, Tennyson dubbing one of these photographs 'The Dirty Monk'. Although one photographic magazine dismissed it as presenting him in such a guise that any bench of magistrates would convict him of being a rogue and vagabond (*Photographic News*, March 1868) Julia was pleased when Henry Taylor said that the picture was as fine as Tennyson's finest poem. She herself thought it an excellent representation of Isaiah or Jeremiah and Tennyson admitted that he liked it better than any other photograph that had been taken of him, bar one – though, despite her scolding, he still frequently refused to sit for her. He disliked the long sessions she required and complained that her many photographs had made him so recognisable that he was now charged double wherever he went. He also said, with displeasure when looking at her work, that 'lines are not ditches'. She used her persuasive powers on him constantly, once showing him the good results she was getting from a negative of him that occupied a large printing frame on the lawn, telling him that if he sat for her again she could make a Rembrandt-like picture of him. He declined.

William Allingham gave an example of the quirky relationship between Julia and Tennyson when, at teatime at the Tennysons, Julia turned up in her usual red openwork shawl with her two young sons. She showed him a small firework toy called Pharaoh's Serpents, which, when lighted, twisted about in a worm-like shape. Julia announced they were poisonous, and Tennyson immediately put out his hand. Julia shrieked at him not to touch: '"You sha'n't, Alfred." But Alfred did. "Wash your hands then!" But Alfred wouldn't and rubbed his moustache instead, enjoying Mrs. C.'s agonies.' She then asked if he'd come to her tomorrow and be photographed. He very emphatically said 'no'.[7]

Allingham had several pressing notes from Julia to come round and bring Dante Gabriel Rossetti with him so that she could 'photograph you both'. But when he asked Rossetti if he would, the reply was also a firm, if brave, refusal. Julia had already been complaining to him about getting people to sit for her. 'I want to do a large photograph of Tennyson, and he objects! Says I make bags under his eyes – and Carlyle refuses to give me a sitting, he says it's a kind of *Inferno*! The *greatest* men of the age, Sir John Herschel, Henry Taylor, Watts, say I have *immortalised* them – and these other men object!! What is one to do – hm?'[8]

Julia was in fact on very good terms with her reluctant sitters, who spoke of (and to) her with exasperated affection. Thomas Carlyle, an agnostic, once, on receiving a Bible anonymously through the post, took one look at it and said that either the Devil or Julia Cameron had sent it to him. Tennyson was more irritated than amused when Julia urged him to sign her photographs of him, aware that they increased in value if he did so. The more he signed, the more she wanted him to sign and on one occasion she turned up at his house with such a large sheaf of them that she had had to take a carriage. She also brought several new pens with her, so he had no excuse for not signing. He greeted her with the words, 'Julia Cameron, Julia Cameron, you are a dreadful woman.'[9] Anne Thackeray noticed that because Tennyson disliked being bothered for his signature like this, Julia thought nothing of the extra labour of forging his signature on the prints. She also wrote to Sir John Herschel in February 1864 to say that it would benefit her commercially if his name could be associated with her work.[10]

About the same time she gave her friends G.F. Watts and Anne Thackeray albums of her photographs, writing the warning on one of them, obviously based on experience, 'Fatal to photographs are cups of tea and coffee, candles and lamps, and children's fingers.'

Julia claimed the first time she exhibited her photographs was in May 1865, but the date was actually May 1864 and the event was the tenth annual exhibition of the Photographic Society of London.

The reviews were mixed. The editor of *Photographic Notes* considered her work was 'Admirable, expressive and vigorous, but dreadfully opposed to photographic conventionalities and proprieties.' He added, covering his back, 'They are more valuable for being so.'[11] The *Photographic News* was more dismissive. 'As one of the special charms of photography consists in the completeness, detail, and finish, we can scarcely commend works in which the aim appears to have been to avoid these qualities. The portraits are chiefly those of men of mark, as artists or authors, and include Mr. Holman Hunt, Mr. Henry Taylor, Mr. G.F. Watts, and some others, and both from the subjects and the mode of treatment, interest while they fail to please us.'[12]

When Lewis Carroll visited this exhibition on 23 June, he said he 'did *not* admire Mrs Cameron's large heads taken out of focus'. The feeling appeared to be mutual. Julia in turn wrote to Henry Taylor to say, 'Your photograph by Dodgson [Carroll] I heard described as looking like "a sea monster fed upon milk". The Tennysons abhor that photograph . . . it has printed so ill – come out so white *and* feeble *and* so grotesque.'[13]

Henry Taylor remarked that few of Julia's photographs were more beautiful than those she had taken of Alice Liddell when the child's father, the Dean of Christchurch, and the rest of his family were staying at Tennyson's house. Carroll might have agreed with another critic who considered these photos of Alice showed her as 'a rather unearthly Pre-Raphaelite heroine, like some golden damozel of a drug-induced fantasy'.[14]

Carroll liked neatness, accuracy and design, while Julia 'intensely courted passion and soul'. However, the two, having circled each other warily, did become reconciled. When Carroll visited the Isle of Wight in July 1864, he called on Julia several times and photographed Ewen, the Camerons' son. Nevertheless, writing to his sister, Louisa, early in August about his visit, he said that when the two of them looked at each other's photographs he saw that Julia had taken all hers deliberately out of focus. This, he thought, sometimes produced a very picturesque effect, while at other times it was 'merely hideous'.

What irritated him was Julia's unswerving conviction that all her photographs were 'triumphs of art'. Indeed, she told Carroll that she only wished she could have had some of *his* subjects to do *out* of focus. He wrote drily to his sister to say that he expressed an analogous wish regarding some of *her* photographs.[15] It had slight overtones of Anne Thackeray's visit to the National Gallery that year with Millais – when he shook his fist at the Raphael *Madonna*.

She also submitted more photographs to an exhibition by the Photographic Society of Scotland, held between December 1864 and March 1865. One was a head of Henry Taylor which, she said, 'had the light illuminating the countenance in a way that cannot be described'; and the other was a Raphaelesque madonna called 'La Madonna Aspettante'. They were not chosen for the prize, which went to a photo called 'Brenda' (a girl sitting reading) by the art photographer, Henry Peach Robinson. Julia said of this picture that it, 'clearly proved to me that detail of table-cover, chair and crinoline skirt were essential to the judges of the art, which was then in its infancy'.[16] Henry Peach Robinson, in turn, disliked her 'out of focus' technique.

So, too, did A.H. Wall, writing in the *Photographic News* in 1865. He thought her idea of artistic photography a curious one which could be described as 'consisting in the main of a piece of light or dark drapery pulled about the figure or over the head of some person in modern costume, which was concealed by much tucking in here and pulling out there, and in the photographing thereof with a lens turned out of focus'. Other hostile critics found her work unreal and complained that it transgressed against photographic naturalism.

The reviewer for the Photographic Society of London's *Journal*, commenting that year on her submissions to the Scottish exhibition, also had little time for her work. She was commended for her 'daring originality', but this was achieved, said the reviewer, 'at the expense of all other photographic qualities. . . . In these pictures all that is good in photography has been neglected, and the shortcomings of the art are prominently exhibited.' The reviewer added, perhaps more patronisingly than benevolently, 'We are sorry to have to speak thus severely on the works of a lady, but we feel compelled to do so in the interests of the art.'[17]

Ladies were expected to know their place – which in the Victorian mid-1860s was at home, stitching samplers. Julia was professionally competitive and ambitious in a male world and the modern critic Sylvia Wolf has paid tribute to her for being 'intellectually engaged with the ideas of her time, not cloistered in her house, childlike and adoring'.[18] Middle-class women were not expected to leave their cloisters and compete financially with men, indeed they were not expected to be involved with finances at all. However, male assumptions were already under siege, and not just by women. It was in 1865 that John Stuart Mill, a strong supporter of female suffrage, was elected to parliament.

Julia admitted that she would have been extremely dispirited by the attack in the *Journal* if she had taken any notice of it. 'It was unsparing and too manifestly unjust for me to attend to it. The more lenient and discerning judges gave me large space upon their walls which seemed to invite the irony and spleen of the printed notice.'[19]

Despite hostile reviews, the year 1865 was a successful one for Julia, particularly considering she had only been working for such a short time. She presented one of her photographs to the British Museum in January ('Fruits of the Spirit') and was delighted when the Victoria and Albert Museum (known as the South Kensington Museum) then bought twenty photographs from her. She contributed to two exhibitions in Berlin, winning a bronze medal the first year and a gold medal the second. She also won an honourable mention in a Dublin exhibition and received a silver medal from the Hartley Institution.

Emily Tennyson had been urging Julia to sell her photographs for some time, even writing letters on her behalf and Julia now signed up with P. & D. Colnaghi and Company, the printmakers in Pall Mall, London, to sell and distribute her photographs. They priced her prints at between 10*s* 6*d* and a guinea. Colnaghi's had opened a photographic department some six years previously, when public demand for prints increased. Julia, a tireless worker, produced 500 negatives between January 1864 and April 1866.

Her confidence in her own work remained strong and she decided to mount her first solo show, which was held at Colnaghi's from November 1865 to January 1866. She was always anxious to get as much (good) publicity as possible for her work, and thought nothing of writing to William Michael Rossetti, whose portrait she had taken, saying rather brashly, 'Have you no means of introducing any friendly Paragraph into any Paper that has *good* circulation?'

William Allingham, a friend of Julia's, went to see her exhibition and said 'I blew the trumpet for it in the *Pall Mall* [*Gazette*]'. His reward was small. On a later visit to the Camerons' house, he noted in his diary that he had to wait a long time for lunch as 'Mrs C. and her household take no note of time'. He saw a group of girls Julia had been photographing going upstairs in fancy dresses, while she greeted him, lunch quite forgotten, carrying a glass negative in her collodionised hands and saying 'Magnificent! To focus them all in one picture, such an effort!'[20]

Strongly disliking enlarged photographs, as she was convinced her photographs would suffer from this difficult and rarely used procedure, Julia instead bought a larger camera in the spring of 1866. It took plates of 15 × 12 inches (her first one having taken plates of 9 × 11). Anne Thackeray commented that both in life and on paper Julia gave herself more space than other people. The larger camera had what was called a 'Rapid

Rectilinear' lens with a 30 in focal length and the combination of the larger plate and this lens prevented distortion in her close-up studies.

She was praised for using this lens by the Victorian photographer P.H. Emerson, as he considered it gave a truer picture than the quicker portrait lenses.[21] However, it also very much reduced the range of sharp focus and the longer focal length required very lengthy exposures. As she wouldn't allow any of her sitters to use a headrest and exposures took from three to seven minutes, her subjects naturally moved very slightly and the result was the 'soft' focus for which she was celebrated. By softening the focus she allowed the realism of the camera to penetrate, as she believed, to the inner spirit.

One of her firm beliefs was her refusal to retouch her photographs as many other professionals did, in order to make them appear rather more flattering to the sitter. In a letter to Sir Edward Ryan about her desire to produce a volume of her photographs, she said 'Lastly as to spots they must I think remain. I could have them touched out but I am *the only* photographer who always issues untouched photographs and artists for this reason amongst others value my photographs.'[22] She followed Watts's advice, which was 'What is, is, and one should not desire to make it seem to be other.' She actually *raised* the price of a print of hers of Henry Taylor on the grounds that an 'accident has happened to negative'.

Retouching was a matter for argument in the photographic press. Like artists, many photographers were willing to flatter their subjects by, say, removing wrinkles or a double chin. Her critics said Julia could not distinguish the gulf between altering features and 'spotting' – i.e. removing spots and scratches on the pictures.

Helmut Gernsheim, in his study of her work, *Julia Margaret Cameron: Her Life and Photographic Work* considered that her lens, her haphazard methods and the resulting damaged surface of many of her photographs caused by uneven development, brought understandable headlong criticism down on her from professional critics and disguised her achievements for the first two years before her methods improved. He considered that 'Mrs Cameron was so obsessed by the spiritual quality of her pictures that she paid too little attention to whether the image was sharp or not, whether the sitter had moved, or whether the plate was covered with blemishes. . . . Lacking training, she had a complete disregard for technical perfection.'

Gernsheim points out that she wrote to Sir John Herschel to say that she hoped to elevate her art beyond 'mere conventional topographic Photography . . . which lacked that modelling of flesh & limb which the focus I use only can give tho' called & condemned as "out of focus." What is focus – & who has a right to say what focus is the legitimate focus?'[23]

Her unprecedented 'out of focus' photographs were explained (at least to his satisfaction) by her youngest son, Henry Herschel, who became a photographer himself. He told his mother that her first successes in her out-of-focus pictures were a fluke because when she focused on an image which to her eye was very beautiful, she stopped there 'instead of screwing on the lens to the more definite focus which all other photographers insist upon'. She said, meekly for her, that his remarks were quite true and was grateful to him for his help over the difficulties of focusing.

Julia's exhibition at Colnaghi's in 1865–6 roused little interest in the photographic press and failed to bring her the attention and financial success she hoped for. But she did at least win a two-page critique by Coventry Patmore (a close friend of her sister Maria) in *Macmillan's Magazine* in 1866, which said that she 'was the first person who had the wit to see that her mistakes were her successes, and henceforward to make her portraits systematically out of focus'. Although he praised the heads she had photographed as being 'beauty of the highest art', he felt she had done herself an injustice by making *pictures* out of her photographs. 'She is not content with putting one or more noble heads or figures on her paper; but she must group them into tableaux vivants, and call them, "Faith, Hope, and Charity", "St Agnes", "The Infant Samuel", "The Salutation, after Giotto", &c.&c. The effect of this is often strange, and sometimes grotesque; and must do much more to diminish the general popularity of the pieces which have such titles than any advantage, in the way of convenience of references, can compensate.'[24]

It is not surprising that Julia was drawn towards *tableaux vivants*. They were in the tradition of Victorian amateur theatricals and Julia was always putting on plays and charades at Freshwater. Most Victorians loved sentiment – look at the popularity of the exhibition of stuffed kittens which portrayed tableaux like 'Who Killed Cock Robin?' and the vast number of printed cards on sale showing waif-like children clasped together, looking heavenwards, under headings like 'The Better Land'.

Admittedly 'artistic' portrayals of children were decidedly not to everyone's taste and over twenty years later, Bernard Shaw, then art critic of the *Star*, commented: 'While the portraits of Herschel, Tennyson and Carlyle beat hollow anything I have ever seen, right on the same wall, and virtually in the same frame, there are photographs of children with no clothes on, or else the underclothes by way of propriety, with palpably paper wings, most inartistically grouped and artlessly labelled as angels, saints or fairies. No-one would imagine that the artist who produced the marvellous Carlyle would have produced such childish trivialities.'[25]

Amanda Hopkinson, in her biography of Julia, observes more perceptively that 'Like many other amateurs, she also photographed women and children; unlike them she developed a form of allegorical representation intended to bestow a translucent relevance on her compositions.'[26] Despite the critics, Julia's enthusiasm, energy and *joie de vivre* were unclouded. Henry Taylor wrote to his daughter on 3 June 1866 with a description of a journey to hell involving Julia, which shows the happy chaos surrounding her, and certainly gives no impression of her being in any way cast down by poor reviews of her work.

Taylor had encountered Julia when travelling back to the Isle of Wight from Waterloo. His luggage had been placed in the carriage of the train and five minutes before the train was due to start he saw Julia, May Prinsep (Thoby Prinsep's niece), a maid and one of Julia's models run down the platform. Julia took her ticket,

> jumped into the carriage – a crowd of people on various errands surrounded the door, to whom she dispensed one after another, with shrieking haste, payment of bills, *douceurs*, cab-hires, fees for messages carried, fees for messages *to be carried* – and then she shrieked to the porter an enquiry how many packages he had received; and he answered 26 had come with her, but there were several waiting before . . . Train started amidst infinite shrieking – model and maid

went second class. Arrived at Brockenhurst – Mrs. C's packages counted out of the van to the number of 39 – transferred to the boat with 39 screams; I squatted on the deck . . . Mrs. C jumped up – ripping open of 'Lady Augusta' imminent [a large cushion known by that name] for inside her was a wrapper. I jump up to save Lady Augusta. Hat blows off – laughter of all beholders . . . arrival . . . carriage filled inside with Mrs Cameron, May Prinsep, self and many precious packages. Model requested to mount the box and demurs . . . arrival . . . model lectured on difference of ranks and introduced to the Madonna and the Beggar-maid as models who were humble and knew their place – model apologizes and declares she objected to the box only from consideration of personal danger and risk of life by tumbling off the coachbox. All right, and the day closes in peace, shrieks dying away in the distance.[27]

Judging from such activity, photography appears to have filled Julia's life, but that year, 1866, Henry Taylor mentioned in a letter that four of his friends were writing novels, Julia being one of them. Taylor said rather damningly that he had not seen her manuscript, nor did he wish to as he did not expect to be able to applaud her work. Her genius, he said, was 'too profuse and redundant, not distinguishing between felicitous and infelicitous – sometimes singing out of the fullest foliage and sometimes taking a long flight to fetch a very small twig'.[28]

Writing was a sideline. Despite the lacklustre results of the Colnaghi exhibition Julia embarked on a further series of exhibitions of her work. She followed up a show in Paris in 1867 with one in London the following year. For the first time her work attracted wide praise from newspapers and magazines. She was so delighted she collected up the reviews and had them reprinted as a pamphlet which she then promptly sent out to her friends. As Pamela Gerrish Nunn comments, in an intriguing book by Nicky Bird tracing the descendants of Julia's models, 'Moderation, modesty, tentativeness and decorum were not the currency she dealt in.'[29]

However, she had every right to be proud. The *Morning Post* thought her photographs were 'unquestionably to be ranked among the very best of their class', attributing their distinctive excellence 'less to the manual expertness than to the refined taste and true artistic feeling of the photographer'.[30] The *Standard*'s reviewer considered her portraits were remarkable for their force and tenderness of expression and a classical effectiveness never seen before in photographs. 'Some remind you of that oft-cited painter Rembrandt: strong light falls full on the face, the shadows around, while dark, possess a transparency which the eye can penetrate. With little regard for details, Mrs. Cameron secures force of expression.' Her compositions were described as very admirable (though the words 'in parts' were added).[31] The words 'artistic taste' jumped out from most reviews.

Julia still looked for – and indeed received – support and praise from her friends. Victor Hugo wrote to her after she sent him some of her work, to say, 'All of them are beautiful, not one of the photographs but is in itself a masterpiece . . . I throw myself at your feet.' George Eliot sent her a warmly appreciative letter and the philosopher Frederick Denison Maurice, to whom she sent some photographs of Tennyson in 1866, replied saying that if they had such portraits of Shakespeare and Milton, 'we should know more of their own selves'.

She was frequently in contact with Watts on the subject of principles of composition, and sometimes recorded his reactions, like 'Quite Divine – G.F. Watts' under the photograph called the 'Dream', based on Milton's dream of his deceased wife, and 'I wish I could paint such a picture as this', under another. His comments delighted her and she said of him that he 'gave me such encouragement that I felt I had wings to fly with'. After seeing one of her photographs of him, he said that he knew of no finer portrait among the Old Masters.

He also commented on the minutiae of her work. Writing to her concerning a new batch of her prints, he said: 'All the heads are divine, and the plates very nearly perfect; the tone too is excellent. If you are going on photographing your grandchild, and he is well worth it, do have a little shirt made of some yellowing material. The blot of formless white spoils the whole picture. What would not do in painting will not do in photography, but otherwise I am delighted with the amount of gradation you have obtained.' In another letter he thanks her for sending some photographs of Tennyson. Some he considered magnificent, others he criticised, telling her to do justice to the poet's 'noble and beautiful head', the finest, he said, she would ever have before her lens.[32] The March issue of the *Photographic News*, which thought her 'wilfully imperfect photography' was 'altogether repulsive', was also exercised about Tennyson, claiming that one of her photographs of him made him look appallingly scruffy. Watts had previously painted an idealised portrait of the Poet Laureate. Julia would have none of this and emphasised the bags under Tennyson's eyes.

Trying to persuade Sir Edward Ryan to use his influence to get a volume of her photographs published, she wrote to him to say that 'Artists, Mr. Watts and Mr. Rossetti, indeed all artists say that mine is the only photography in the world which gives them pure unmixed delight. Du Maurier says "it *charms* me" and all speak in this tone of my work.' A letter from Sir John Herschel must also have confirmed her confidence in herself, starting as it did: 'This last batch of your photographs is indeed wonderful in two distinct lines of perfection.' He made some critical points but ended, 'altogether you seem resolved to out-do yourself on every fresh effort'.[33]

Julia, now fifty-four, continued to exhibit widely: in 1869 she showed in the Netherlands; then again in London in 1870, followed by twice at the London International Exhibition – in 1871 and 1872. Yet still financial success eluded her. A friend, writing to Tennyson's brother in 1873, mentioned her prints being on sale at Colnaghi's and said, 'but I fear it is not a successful speculation – as to money. She is not likely to make money as a photographer, or indeed in any way. She is too orientally magnificent and generous in her ideas.'[34]

That Julia was intent on making money from her photography only further annoyed the photographic establishment, already critical of what they considered her slapdash methods. Many were either loath to praise her achievements, or could not recognise them as such, and scoffed at her results. They failed to realise that the greatest British pictorial photographer of the age had emerged.

EIGHT

'I WANT A FACE WELL WORN WITH EVIL PASSION'

As Watts became progressively less interested in portraits he played an important part in convincing Julia that allegorical composition was the highest form of art. She was already far ahead of many of her contemporaries in her imaginative and unconventional treatment of subjects. With her love of beauty, she was also influenced by the paintings of friends who were prime movers in the pre-Raphaelite movement. Roger Fry, the art critic, wrote that Pre-Raphaelitism had 'leavened the cultured society of the day with an extraordinary passion for beauty. . . . The cult of beauty was a religion. . . . The devotees of this creed cultivated the exotic and precious with all the energy and determination of a dominant class. . . . They openly admitted to being "intense".'[1] Apart from her love of beauty, Julia was genuinely interested in allegory and myth and tried in her own photographs to imitate the poetic and pictorial symbolism of the

Pre-Raphaelites. This was not always successful. One critic of Victorian photography scorned those who were 'posing and draping their models and backgrounds as for a pantomime', and added that Julia was guilty of an error of taste when 'imbued with the sentiments of her intellectual friends [she] devoted an important part of her time to the creation of an absurdity which we may describe as "Pre-Raphaelite photography".'[2]

Gernsheim made the point that though Julia sometimes posed her sitters in similar attitudes to those used by the Pre-Raphaelites, she was more akin to Dante Gabriel Rossetti than any of the others. 'Many of her women have the strange emotional quality and melancholy expression so often found in Rossetti's faces.'[3]

There was immense and growing interest in art at the time, which resulted in a huge vogue for etchings and engravings of well-known paintings by the Pre-Raphaelites and others. These were on sale in many London shops while prints and photographs, equally popular, were sold at print makers like Colnaghi's. It was a great period for illustrated books and painters like Millais were commissioned to do woodcuts for these – woodcuts being the favoured method for reproduction. Dante Gabriel Rossetti and Holman Hunt were two of the Pre-Raphaelite painters asked to produce woodcuts to illustrate Tennyson's *Poems*.

In 1871 the lease of Little Holland House was up and, though extended for two years, the Prinseps and Watts finally had to leave. Watts had bought some land at Freshwater and was at last able to return thirty years of hospitality. He had a cottage-cum-villa built there called 'The Briary' and he and the Prinseps moved in. Julia was delighted to have them as neighbours. Although she still devoted most of her time to photographs – the Tennysons' younger son Lionel was one of her favourite subjects – she was also enthusiastically producing amateur plays, a long-time love. A reproduction of one of her playbills is headed: 'Amateur Theatricals. At Mrs. Cameron's Thatched House'.[4] As critical in her role of producer as photographer, she once demolished her son's performance with the words, 'Oh heavens, Henry, do you call that making love? Here let *me* show you how to do it.'

The year 1873 was successful professionally for Julia – she exhibited at the Universal Exhibition, Vienna, and the International Exhibition in London – but it was a devastating one personally. Visiting Emily Tennyson in the spring she refused everything but some bread and champagne and then had a dizzy fit. Emily said, 'It was not much . . . but the state of alarm it threw her into was most pitiable. Her poor nerves are thoroughly shattered.'[5] This was hardly surprising. Her son Charles had been ill for a long time and had recently had a serious operation to remove part of his jawbone.

Meanwhile her son Henry, who was dabbling around acting, was a further worry to her. If he failed in a stage career, he would have to go out to Ceylon and work on the family estate – a thought Julia disliked as he was a great comfort to her. As Emily said, he 'soothes and manages her beautifully'. Nevertheless, he left that year for Ceylon.

But the greatest blow to Julia was the death in childbirth, in October of that year, of her adored and only daughter, Julia. Married to Charles Norman, she had already borne six children. Her mother had taken surprisingly few photographs of her, her favourite family model being her niece Julia Jackson. Bereft, she wrote to Sir Edward Ryan to say that their Christmas gathering was and would be forever saddened by the death of her firstborn.

It must have helped distract her when, in August 1874, Tennyson suggested to Julia that she provide a set of photographs to illustrate his *Idylls of the King and Other Poems*, which was about to be republished by Henry King as a twelve-volume set in a popular Cabinet Edition. In a letter to Sir Edward Ryan she said she told Tennyson that she consented – as it was 'immortality' to her to be bound up with him. She admitted to Tennyson that 'although I bully you I have a corner of worship for you in my heart'.[6]

Henry Taylor once said of Tennyson that 'He wants a story to treat, being full of poetry with nothing to put it in.' *The Idylls*, which were based on the legends of King Arthur and his knights of the round table, solved this problem and had proved incredibly popular. Julia's great-niece, Laura Troubridge, recalled the way people discussed it by the hour, weeping over Elaine's ill-starred love for Lancelot, arguing as to whether Geraint should have taken so mean an advantage of the patience of his wife; speaking solemnly of the death of Arthur and Guinevere's guilty love.

Julia was immediately fired by the idea, having, like the Pre-Raphaelites, always been inspired by Tennyson's romantic legendary poetry. Her translation of the narrative poem *Leonora* published in 1847 showed her long-term interest in such verse.

> Leonora from an anxious dream
> Starts up at break of day:
> 'My William, art thou false or slain?
> Oh! William, why delay?'

She had, over the years, taken various narrative photographs, calling them 'Fancy Subjects for Pictorial Effect' and acknowledged her debt to the photographer David Wilkie Wynfield, who used to photograph his friends in Renaissance costume. She wrote to William Michael Rossetti back in 1864 to say: 'to my feelings about his [Wynfield's] beautiful Photography I owed *all* my attempts and indeed consequently all my success.'[7]

Una Taylor recalled the stream of different costumes and characters featuring in the photographs. 'Sitters, issuing from the big wooden annexes which served Julia Margaret Cameron as a photographic studios, attired in garments cast over them by the imperious artist, shawls of Indian embroideries, flowing robes, or it might be mimic panoplies of mail, wandered in the garden . . . there were maid servants transformed into Madonnas . . . Henry Taylor crowned with tinsel diadem, enacting the part of King Lear . . . while old Charles Cameron held the oar of the dumb boatman, whose barge bore the Lady of Shalott down the slow-flowing river between the reeds to Camelot.'[8]

With *The Idylls*, Julia was to begin work in earnest on such 'Fancy Subjects'. The project was to exhaust her, despite her enthusiasm and superabundant energy. She had very little time to complete it (publication of the first volume was to be in the December of that year, a mere three months after she was first asked to contribute). In that time she had to set up the scenes illustrating the text and find the requisite models, props and costumes.

She found it particularly difficult to find the right models, especially one for the adulterer Lancelot in 'The Parting of Sir Lancelot and Queen Guinevere' (a parting necessary after King Arthur's wife had fallen in love with his knight, Lancelot) and only found one very late in the day. Wilfred Ward, the son of the eminent Victorian theologian 'Ideal Ward', recalled her bringing Tennyson to his father's house around this time and calling out, immediately she saw Cardinal Vaughan – to whom she was a perfect stranger – 'Alfred, I have found Sir Lancelot', only to have Tennyson, unaware of the Cardinal's identity, reply 'I want a face well worn with evil passion.'[9]

Practically any passer-by was pressed into service. Julia's great-niece said that no tourist was safe from her. 'Men and women gazing quietly at the sea or walking down the dusty lanes that zigzagged between flowering hedges, were liable to find themselves bidden in a way that brooked no denial into her studio, where, a few moments later, they would find themselves posing as Geraint, or Enid, Lancelot or Guinevere.'[10] In the interests of art, she could be ruthless.

One girl remembered the agony of sitting for so long: 'The exposure began. A minute went over and I felt as if I must scream; another minute, and the sensation was as if my eyes were coming out of my head; a third, and the back of my neck appeared to be afflicted with palsy; a fourth, and the crown, which was too large, began to slip down my forehead.'[11] At the end, Julia merely said she was afraid the girl had moved. Wanting her models to look virginal, she no doubt repeated the brisk advice her great-niece said she gave her young female relations: 'If ever you fall into temptation, down on your knees, and think of Aunt Julia.'

Julia commandeered William Warder, a porter from Yarmouth pier, to impersonate King Arthur, and his fine, noble appearance was approved of by Tennyson. Looking for a model for Queen Guinevere, Julia spotted a young woman who was on vacation at Freshwater, took her to lunch and persuaded her to be photographed. The verse from *The Idylls* that she was illustrating was:

> He [King Arthur] paused, and in the pause she crept
>   an inch
> Nearer, and laid her hands about his feet.

When a friend of the model saw her later on, looking tired, she asked if perhaps she'd been on a long walk. The girl's explanation was simple. She had been lying on the floor for the last two hours, clutching the porter's ankle.

Another unknown young woman, also staying at Freshwater, was approached by Julia but needed a great deal of persuasion to be photographed in the character of 'Vivien' (an enchantress who lived in a palace in the middle of a magic lake) as she did not consider her a 'nice' person. To her further dismay, she found that Mr Cameron was to represent Merlin. Her objection was nothing to do with Charles Cameron as a man, but she had heard he was subject to fits of hilarity and was worried he might laugh in the part.

And laugh he did. He was to be photographed sitting inside a hollow fragment of oak tree covered in ivy leaves – a scene which took the gardener half a day to arrange in the studio. Julia started the exposure, but the girl posing as Vivien said that 'it was more than mortal could stand to see the oak beginning gently to vibrate, and know that the extraordinary phenomenon was produced by the suppressed chuckling of Merlin'. She admitted that the first two negatives of her were a total failure, though she managed to hold steady for the third. However, Merlin had moved far too much. 'There were at least fifty Merlins to be seen. With an "Oh Charles, Charles", half good-natured and half reproachful, Mrs Cameron gave Merlin up, at least for that day. I believe that the amiable old gentleman was always sitting for Merlin, that is to say, as often as a suitable Vivien could be found.'[12]

Despite Julia's dictatorial methods, she was so enthusiastic, so energetic, so direct and so ready to help others that those she encountered found her endearing.

There was an ongoing argument at the time as to whether illustrations should merely form an 'overture' to the text, or be realistic. Many book illustrators of the time chose to give a very realistic, exact version of the text – like F. Barnard's drawings for the Household Edition of Charles Dickens's work. Checked against the text, every bit of apparel, every expression, is exactly as described. Julia wanted to express poetic realism, and she wrote to the Bristol Art Society when her illustrations to the *Idylls of the King* were published to say that Tennyson was pleased with her 'ideal representation' of the idylls.

So, too, were the publishers of the new edition. On first seeing Julia's photographs in October 1874, they wrote to congratulate her on her 'wonderful, wonderful, past all whooping' photographs. King Arthur they thought 'magnificent', Merlin was 'grand', and Elaine unbelievably beautiful. But when the first volume of the *Idylls of the King* was published the following month, Julia, although knowing her photographs – copied as woodcuts – would be reduced in size, was still upset to see how small they were. She had taken the photographs, she said, for friendship and fame, but was nevertheless anxious to make a commercial success. Tennyson, she knew, had earned a great deal from the *Idylls*.

She told Sir Edward Ryan how she felt, particularly after taking 'my beautiful large pictures at such a cost of labour, strength & money, for I have taken 245 photographs to get these 12 successes'. Tennyson suggested she publish them (at her own risk) in actual size in a big volume. She did so, producing the illustrations separately in January 1875, together with the passages they referred to – which she had copied out in her own handwriting. The cost was six guineas, though the photographs could be bought singly. Later she published a further volume of twelve more illustrations as well as a miniature edition.

She worked hard to publicise her work, sending the books to art societies and writing to friends like Alick Wedderburn, Ruskin's biographer, asking if they could help with publicity. But as Violet Hamilton, in her book *Annals of My Glasshouse: Photographs by Julia Margaret Cameron*, points out, 'the publication was neither a great commercial success nor did her illustrations receive the critical acclaim which she expected. During her lifetime the photographic press condemned almost all her work; the art critics preferred her portraits to the "fancy subjects".'[13]

The photographs for *The Idylls* were to be Julia's last major work. It was 1875. Her husband was now eighty years old and pined for his beloved Ceylon, for the monkeys and the elephants among whom he had 'once lived as a brother'. He admitted to Sir Henry Taylor that he had long contemplated the country as his final resting place. His health had been deteriorating and it had confined him to walking around his own garden in a picturesque blue and crimson dressing gown.

With his health and happiness in mind, and her own wish to see her four sons who were working out there, Julia agreed to leave England and go to Ceylon to live. In triumph, Charles Cameron borrowed a coat from Hardinge, his one son still in England, and for the first time in twelve years, left the house and walked down to the seashore.

NINE

A LITTLE HUT WITH MUD WALLS

The Camerons initially kept their decision to go and live in Ceylon a secret from their friends – in Henry Taylor's opinion to avoid discussion and expostulation. But when they announced that they were leaving for Ceylon to be with their sons (Hardinge was travelling with them) their friends and relatives at Freshwater and elsewhere were predictably horrified. Those who went to Dimbola to say goodbye found the place in a turmoil: packing cases were piled up everywhere and telegrams poured in and out.

The crowds of their friends who went to the ship at Southampton in October 1875 to see them off found equal chaos there. Porters were scurrying past carrying large white mounting boards used for photographs; Charles Cameron was wandering around with a carved ivory cane in one hand and, in the other, a pink rose given to him by Lady Tennyson as a parting gift; Julia was bestowing affectionate goodbyes on friends in between shouting instructions about innumerable packages and persuading a nervous cow up the gangway

– a present from her sister, Virginia, to ensure they had fresh milk on board. There were also two coffins, filled temporarily with glass and china – to ensure a decent burial. Charles Cameron had long decided on the site of his tomb in Ceylon (which was not, in the end, where he was buried).

Running out of English currency to tip the army of waiting porters who had transferred all their goods to the ship, Julia instead handed out copies of her mounted photographs. Their reaction is unknown. She also generously endowed the walls of the railway station waiting rooms of Lymington and Brockenhurst with her photographs. The negatives of her photographs she placed with a firm of photographic printers, the Autotype Company. They agreed to make prints of any portraits that interested the public, though the arrangement foundered when Julia discovered that they charged a 40 per cent commission.

During the voyage to Ceylon, she wrote to Emily Tennyson to say that amid the bustling world of 380 people on board, her husband sat there majestically, like a being from another sphere, 'his white hair shining like the foam of the sea and his white hands holding on each side his golden chain'. Julia loved the way everything glittered: the sapphire sea, the pearl-white houses, the emerald and ruby boats. But it was a hard voyage. They had to endure the gales of the Bay of Biscay and the heat of the Red Sea. In another letter to Anne Thackeray she wrote at length of being virtually battened down below the hatches during bad weather. On arrival at Colombo in Ceylon, she presented the Captain of the ship with a harmonium – she'd raised a subscription from the passengers to pay for this – in gratitude for a safe journey.

She showed immense fortitude and humour, writing to Emily Tennyson to say: 'Think of us in a little hut with only mud walls, four hundred feet above the level of the sea.'[1] Typically, with courage and enthusiasm, she embraced the new life stretching ahead of her: living in a mountain house at Kalutara, south of Colombo above the sea (rather grander than a mud hut). It was surrounded by coconut and breadfruit trees, mangoes and casuarinas and was a haven for rabbits, squirrels and mynah birds. A tame stag kept guard at the open door and grey-whiskered monkeys wandered around outside.

Julia was an extraordinary woman. She never repined, at least not openly, about the dramatic change in her life: the abrupt ending of her power-drive for photography, her ambition, her talent. She showed no resentment at this, or at having to leave behind in England her dearest friends like Tennyson, Taylor and Watts. She was simply glad to see her sons, glad her husband was happy – and unaware or uncaring of the great cost to herself. She didn't give up photography entirely, taking a series of portraits of plantation and other workers, but the main thrust and achievement of her work – which had lasted only twelve years – was finished.

The move was also at some cost to her health. On arrival in Ceylon, she became ill, telling Emily Tennyson that she thought it was due to all the angst involved in planning and undertaking the journey to Ceylon, and the anguish of some of the partings. She wrote frequently to her friends in England and they were equally responsive. Hearing from Henry Taylor that he had visited the Isle of Wight, which reminded her how much she missed it, she replied in a letter dated May 1876, 'Let the Island be hung with black, yet it sends me all its sweets', telling him her beloved Mrs Tennyson often wrote to her from her sick bed; that Mary Bretherton's 'most delicious' letters came every week; that Anny Thackeray 'out of her broken heart sends a few words now and then'; and that she had just had two from Alfred, 'who tells me all, signing "V. old friend" . . . but Sarah never!!' Her sister, she said, was too encumbered by home cares.

Much of her letter is taken up with the extreme climate: 'I only hope I shall have strength of body, elasticity of spirits and bravery of heart eno' to stand it.' She knew it was good for those who suffered from bronchitis and asthma, but she had heard dreadful accounts of the big monsoon, admitting that even the little monsoon had struck awe into her. 'Sheets of water falling day & night, night & day & with them a *white darkness* over all the land.' This had eclipsed her 'darling mountains' and her Temple, and her ever-changing sky, resulting in a thunderstorm which shook the heavens. Thirty inches of rain had fallen in fifteen days. Her husband, she said, who was very well, continued to assert that even the deluges of a Ceylon monsoon were better than the 'dry delights of a summer sun in dear old England'. She herself still missed England, saying that when Easter day and Easter services had begun, 'in my heart an aching longing began also'. She told him she spent several hours each day reading and had now finished all the works of Sophocles in translation. Her letter ended with the admission she had not been well.[2]

After she had been exactly a year in Ceylon, she wrote to an unknown correspondent to say that her health had benefited from being there, whereas for eight months of the year in England, 'I was never secure against sudden and dangerous attacks of Bronchitis – such illnesses and ailments are unknown in this sunny land, where East winds are not spoken of and coughs and catarrh never heard.' According to her letter, the better climate, the 'glorious beauty of the scenery – the primitive simplicity of the inhabitants' had increased her admiration for Ceylon. Her 81-year-old husband, she said, had also benefited from the climate and was far stronger, 'having been when in England for the previous years in a condition of apathy almost amounting to torpor'. She was delighted with his progress: 'now he walks and rides with vigour and ease and not only reads for several consecutive hours but converses with all the brilliance as to repartee and memory, as to anecdote and quotation, for which he was remarkable in the prime of his life'.[3]

Between 1876 and 1877 Marianne North, the English botanic artist who travelled the world in her quest to discover and paint colourful and exotic flowers, went to Ceylon and, at Julia's pressing invitation, stayed with the Camerons. She was captivated by their house on the hill, jutting out above a river which in turn ran into the sea a quarter of a mile or so below the house. It was splendidly untidy and picturesque. Inside, the walls, tables, chairs and floors were covered with Julia's magnificent photographs and there were quantities of books everywhere. Julia wore a lace veil on her head and flowing draperies and was her usual generous self. When Marianne admired a wonderful grass-green shawl she was wearing, Julia told her it would just suit her, took a pair of scissors, cut it in half from corner to corner and gave one half to her. Meanwhile Charles walked up and down the verandah with his long staff in his hand, white hair flowing over his shoulders, ready to enjoy every joke, every conversation around him. While Marianne was painting he read aloud to her or quoted poetry.

She found Julia had 'a most fascinating and caressing manner, and was full of clever talk and originality'. She insisted on photographing Marianne and this put her in a fever of excitement for three days. In sitting for her,

Marianne experienced the same kind of discomfort that earlier English models had learned to expect. Julia having dressed her up in heavy draperies of cashmere wool, 'she let down my hair and made me stand with spiky coconut branches running into my head, the noonday sun's rays dodging my eyes between the leaves'. With the thermometer standing at 96°F, Julia told her to look perfectly natural. For a second pose, she placed Marianne against a background of breadfruit leaves and fruit, nailed flat against a window shutter and proceeded to tell *them* to look natural too. They failed to heed her. In all, she wasted twelve plates, only getting a likeness, as Marianne admitted ruefully, of a thoroughly uninteresting, commonplace person.

Julia also photographed some local people and, to Marianne's amusement, 'She took such a fancy to the back of one of them (which she said was absolutely superb) that she insisted on her son retaining him as her gardener, though she had no garden and he did not know even the meaning of the word.'[4]

Writing to Henry Taylor in July 1877, Julia said she had so much to tell him about, she scarcely knew where to begin – 'not of news, for our life is one of most acceptable monotony . . . as for excitements – when our hens have hatched their chickens, or a cow has calved, the household is in a stir. . . . On the one day of the week that the English mail comes in there is an awakening. I jump up, seize hold of the brown tin box, hung by a leather strap over the shoulder of my little ebon Mercury – say to E. [her English maid, Ellen Ottington] rapidly "Give him [the Tappal post boy] a present", and empty my box.'[5]

In the spring of 1878, Julia and Charles made a surprise trip to England. It was only to be for a month, 'a month of happiness' wrote Julia to Anne Thackeray's cousin, from the steamer *Poonah* off Malta, on their way to England. Her neice, Julia Jackson, on the other hand, said it was 'a visit of turmoil, sickness, sorrows, marriages and deaths'. Julia was to marry Leslie Stephen that year and their children would include Virginia (who married Leonard Woolf) and Vanessa (who married Clive Bell).

The Camerons expected to arrive on 26 April and Julia thanked God that her husband was well despite the bad weather they had had over the last two weeks. As they no longer had their house at Freshwater, they stayed in London and 'in divine frenzy' saw as many of their old friends as possible. Although Julia was as vital and vigorous as ever, she was warned that her health would not withstand her returning to the heat of Ceylon. But she could not contemplate being separated from her husband and sons. As she said, 'Where your heart is, there is your treasure also.'

England, too, may have had less appeal to her. She was devoted to her sisters, but by now they had all dispersed. Thoby Prinsep had died the previous year and his wife Sarah had virtually collapsed without him – going to live in Brighton, consoling herself by turning to religion and extravagantly spending money on helping the Church. She showed a vestige of the Pattle vivacity when a cousin, on her son's instructions, told her to economise by confining her enthusiastic telegram-sending to one a week and using postcards instead. As soon as the cousin left, Sarah Prinsep wrote telegram after telegram to all her relations describing his visit.[6]

Another sister, Maria Jackson, and her husband, lived near to Sarah. It was their daughter, Julia, who was photographed several times by her aunt Julia, and had married Herbert Duckworth, then Leslie Stephen. Sophia, the youngest sister, was living with her husband and children in Scotland; Louisa, though living in England for years with her family, never seemed to play much part in her sisters' lives; and the beautiful Virginia, Countess Somers, had retired to Aix-les-Bains in the south of France.

When the Camerons returned to Ceylon, they went to live with their son Hardinge, now Government agent, at his residency in the coastal town of Kalutara. Julia took occasional photographs, concentrating on the local workers in the area. But within a few months Hardinge became ill, much of it due to overwork, and he and his parents moved up to his brother Henry's bungalow in the cooler mountain district. Here, in January 1879, Julia caught a chill and was ill for ten days.

Her bed faced a wide-open window and the evening of 26 January 1879 was a glorious one, the night sky full of enormous stars. She looked out, said the one word, 'Beautiful', and died.[7] Her body, covered in a white cloth, was taken by an open cart drawn by two white bullocks for nearly ten miles to the tiny churchyard of St Mary's at Bogawantalawa high up in the mountains – aptly described, which Julia would have appreciated, as 'a dream of beauty'. It was a scene she would surely have wanted to photograph. Tennyson's younger son Lionel wrote to Julia's son Henry, when he heard the news, to say they would never see her like again. Another friend said that the whole world felt the colder and darker for her leaving it. The following year her husband also died and was buried in the same churchyard.

Julia Cameron was only sixty-three years old at her death, comparatively young by today's standards. She had no regrets: she knew the body of her work was accomplished; she was proud of her achievements; and she was surrounded by her sons and adored husband. The obituary in *The Times* said, with truth, 'Mrs Cameron's singular ardour of enthusiasm, the energy with which she flung herself into whatever she undertook, her rare forgetfulness of self and readiness to help others, endeared her to a wide circle of friends.'[8]

The extraordinary quality and power of her photographs went mainly unrecognised by the wider public during her lifetime. Contemporary photographers and critics considered her eccentric rather than talented and her innovative techniques provoked more hostility than praise. Her narrative studies were less well regarded than her portraits, yet she applied the same ruthless perfectionism towards them.

For more than a century after her death her photographs were virtually ignored and forgotten. There are tales of her original prints being sold for a song at jumble sales between the two World Wars and a rinsing sink of hers turned up in a field, being used as a container to feed cattle. As late as 1989 the local authority in the Isle of Wight gave its permission to demolish the 'Cameron House' side of the Dimbola property. Local enthusiasts formed the Julia Margaret Cameron Trust and, with international help, successfully prevented this. They also purchased the remaining half of the property and Dimbola Lodge is now open to the public, with rooms restored and a permanent collection of her work on view.[9]

A steady flow of exhibitions have helped rediscover and recognise Julia's unrivalled skill. It is impossible to be passive about her work. Looking at it today, her enthusiasm and passion still shine out.

NOTES

CHAPTER ONE

1. Elizabeth F. Boyd, 'The Pattle Sisters' (MSS, Rutgers University, New Jersey, USA).
2. Bengal Kalendar, 1800, p. 5.
3. H.G. Keene, *A Servant of 'John Company'* (W. Thacker & Co. 1897), p. 67.
4. M.S. Watts, *George Frederic Watts* (Macmillan & Co., 1912), vol. 1, p. 129.
5. Ethel Smyth, *Impressions that Remained* (Longman, Green & Co., 1919), p. 251.

CHAPTER TWO

1. Brian Hill, *Julia Margaret Cameron: A Victorian Family Portrait* (Peter Owen, 1973), p. 45.
2. Sir Henry Cotton, *Indian and Home Memories* (Fisher Unwin, 1911), p. 53.
3. Bodleian Library, MSS, Eng. Letts, D12, ff. 396–7.
4. Emily Eden, *Up the Country* (R. Bentley, 1866), p. ix.
5. British Library, MSS ADD 40127, f. 85, 22 June 1842.
6. Ibid., ff. 177–86, 7 September 1843.
7. Ibid.
8. Ibid.
9. Ibid., f. 233, 6 December 1844.
10. Ibid., ff. 299–303, 9 February 1845.
11. Smyth, *Impressions that Remained*, p. 251.

CHAPTER THREE

1. British Library, MSS ADD 40127, ff. 177–86, 7 September 1843.

Notes

2. Hill, *Julia Margaret Cameron*, p. 42.
3. Lady Ritchie, *From Friend to Friend* (John Murray, 1920), p. 3.
4. Kathleen Fitzpatrick, *Lady Somerset* (Jonathan Cape, 1923), p. 13.
5. Una Taylor, *Guests and Memories* (Oxford University Press, 1924), p. 217.
6. Fitzpatrick, *Lady Somerset*, p. 14.
7. Ibid., p. 16.
8. Watts, *George Frederic Watts*, p. 204.
9. Lady Ritchie, *From Friend to Friend*, p. 3.

CHAPTER FOUR

1. Charles Tennyson, *Alfred Tennyson* (Macmillan, 1949), p. 323.
2. Bodleian Library, MSS Eng. Letts. CI, 13 February 1850.
3. Henry Taylor, *Autobiography* (Longman, Green, & Co, 1885), vol. 1, p. 53.
4. Ibid., p. 54.
5. Taylor, *Guests and Memories*, p. 201.
6. James O. Hoge (ed.), *Lady Tennyson's Journal* (University Press of Virginia, 1981), p. 21.
7. Watts, *George Frederic Watts*, p. 205.
8. Taylor, *Guests and Memories*, p. 221.
9. Lady Ritchie, *From Friend to Friend*, p.23.
10. Ibid., p. 4.
11. Hester Thackeray Fuller and Violet Hammersley, *Thackeray's Daughter* (Dublin: Euphorion Books, 1951), p. 110.
12. Julia Margaret Cameron, *Annals of My Glasshouse,* in Helmut Gernsheim, *Julia Margaret Cameron: Her Life and Photographic Work* (Gordon Fraser, 1975), p. 182.
13. Watts, *George Frederic Watts*, p. 177.
14. Lady Ritchie, *From Friend to Friend*, p. 5.
15. Colin Ford, *The Cameron Collection: An Album of Photographs by Julia Margaret Cameron Presented to Sir John Herschel* (Van Nostrand Reinhold Co. in association with the National Portrait Gallery, 1975), p. 10.
16. Taylor, *Guests and Memories*, p. 3.

Notes

CHAPTER FIVE

1. Wilfrid Blunt, *England's Michelangelo: a Biography of George Frederic Watts* (Hamish Hamilton, 1975), p. 133.
2. Lady Ritchie, *From Friend to Friend*, p. 28.
3. Watts, *George Frederic Watts*, p. 206.
4. Agnes Grace Weld, *Glimpses of Tennyson and of Some of his Relations and Friends* (Williams & Norgate, 1903), p. 72.
5. Lady Ritchie, *From Friend to Friend*, p. 20.
6. Fuller and Hammersley, *Thackeray's Daughter*, p. 111.
7. Wilfrid Ward, *Men and Matters* (Longman, 1914), p. 257.
8. Fuller and Hammersley, *Thackeray's Daughter*, p. 109.
9. Taylor, *Autobiography*, vol. 2, p. 195.
10. Lady Ritchie, *From Friend to Friend*, p. 24.
11. Brian Hinton, *Immortal Faces: Julia Margaret Cameron on the Isle of Wight* (Isle of Wight County Press and Isle of Wight County Council, 2001), p. 34.
12. Hoge, *Lady Tennyson's Journal*, p. 143.
13. Gernsheim, *Julia Margaret Cameron*, p. 23.
14. Bodleian Library, MSS Eng. Letts 178, 18 July 1862.
15. Ann Thwaite, *Emily Tennyson: the Poet's Wife* (Faber & Faber, 1996), p. 347.
16. Hill, *Julia Margaret Cameron*, p. 98.

CHAPTER SIX

1. Laura Troubridge, *Memories and Reflections* (Heinemann, 1925), p. 34.
2. Andrew Wheatcroft, *The Tennyson Album* (Routledge & Kegan Paul, 1980), p. 102.
3. Cameron, *Annals of My Glasshouse*, p. 181.
4. Violet Hamilton (ed.), *Annals of My Glasshouse: Photographs by Julia Margaret Cameron* (Ruth Chandler Williamson Gallery, Scripps College in association with University of Washington Press, 1996), p. 31.
5. Troubridge, *Memories and Reflections*, p. 35.
6. Ford, *The Cameron Collection*, p. 20.
7. Cameron, *Annals of My Glasshouse*, p. 181.

8. Hamilton, *Annals of My Glasshouse*, p. 18.

9. Hill, *Julia Margaret Cameron*, p. 135.

10. William Crawford, *The Keepers of Light: A History & Working Guide to Early Photographic Processes* (Morgan & Morgan, 1979), p. 42.

11. Watts, *George Frederic Watts*, p. 206.

12. Ellen Terry, *The Story of My Life* (Boydell Press, 1982), p. 35.

13. Ellen Terry Museum, Smallhythe Place, Kent, MSS.

14. Cameron, *Annals of My Glasshouse*, p. 181.

15. Hamilton, *Annals of My Glasshouse*, pp. 31, 28.

16. Cameron, *Annals of My Glasshouse*, p. 183.

17. Sylvia Wolf, *Focus: Five Women Photographers* (A. Whitman, 1994), p. 24.

18. Ian Jeffrey, *Photography: A Concise History* (Thames & Hudson, 1981), p. 40.

19. Cameron, *Annals of My Glasshouse*, p. 182.

20. Lady Ritchie, *From Friend to Friend*, p. 27.

CHAPTER SEVEN

1. Gernsheim, *Julia Margaret Cameron*, p. 30.

2. Virginia Woolf, *Freshwater: A Comedy* (Harcourt Inc, 1976), p. 5.

3. Fuller and Hammersley, *Thackeray's Daughter*, p. 110.

4. Troubridge, *Memories and Reflections*, p. 34.

5. Robert Bernard Martin, *Tennyson, The Unquiet Heart* (Faber & Faber, 1980), p. 449.

6. Gernsheim, *Julia Margaret Cameron*, p. 35.

7. H. Allingham and D. Radford (eds), *William Allingham, A Diary* (Macmillan, 1907), p. 127.

8. Ibid., p. 153.

9. Weld, *Glimpses of Tennyson*, p. 76.

10. Royal Society, Sir John Herschel correspondence, 20 February 1864.

11. *Photographic Notes*, IX (1864), p. 171.

12. *Photographic News* (1864), p. 266.

13. Morton N. Cohen, *The Letters of Lewis Carroll* (Macmillan, 1979), vol. 1, *1837–1885*, p. 54.

Notes

14. Colin Gordon, *Beyond the Looking Glass* (Hodder & Stoughton, 1944), p. 122.
15. Cohen, *The Letters of Lewis Carroll*, p. 66.
16. Cameron, *Annals of My Glasshouse*.
17. Photographic Society of London, *Journal* (February 1865), p. 196.
18. Wolf, *Focus: Five Women Photographers*, p. 48.
19. Cameron, *Annals of My Glasshouse*, p. 181.
20. Allingham and Radford, *William Allingham*, p. 182.
21. P.H. Emerson, *Naturalistic Photography* (Sampson Low, Marston, Searle & Rivington, 1890), p. 152.
22. Gernsheim, *Julia Margaret Cameron*, p. 47.
23. Ibid., p. 70.
24. 'Mrs Cameron's Photographs', *Macmillan's Magazine*, XIII (November 1865 to April 1866), p. 230.
25. Gernsheim, *Julia Margaret Cameron*, p. 67.
26. Amanda Hopkinson, *Julia Margaret Cameron* (Virago, 1986), p. 1.
27. Taylor, *Guests and Memories*, p. 216.
28. Ibid., p. 225.
29. Nicky Bird, *Tracing Echoes* (Wild Pansy Press, 2001), p. 13.
30. *Morning Post*, 29 January 1868.
31. *Standard*, 1 February 1868.
32. Watts, *George Frederic Watts*, p. 207.
33. Cameron, *Annals of My Glasshouse*.
34. Thwaite, *Emily Tennyson*, p. 495.

CHAPTER EIGHT

1. Tristram Powell (ed.), *Victorian Photographs of Famous Men and Fair Women: Julia Margaret Cameron* (Hogarth Press, 1973), p. 24.
2. Alex Strasser, *Victorian Photography* (Focal Press, 1942), p. 60.
3. Gernsheim, *Julia Margaret Cameron*, p. 78.
4. Ford, *The Cameron Collection*, p. 14.
5. Thwaite, *Emily Tennyson*, p. 495.
6. Wolf, *Focus: Five Women Photographers*, p. 87.
7. Gernsheim, *Julia Margaret Cameron*, p. 35.
8. Taylor, *Guests and Memories*, p. 214.
9. Fuller and Hammersley, *Thackeray's Daughter*, p. 113.

10. Troubridge, *Memories and Reflections*, p. 35.
11. 'A Reminiscence of Mrs Cameron by a Lady Amateur', *Photographic News* (1 January 1886).
12. Ibid.
13. Hamilton, *Annals of My Glasshouse*, p. 59.

CHAPTER NINE

1. Fuller and Hammersley, *Thackeray's Daughter*, p. 117.
2. Bodleian Library, MSS Eng. Lett. D.13 f. 81.
3. *Whisper of the Muse: The Overstone Album and Other Photographs by Julia Margaret Cameron* (Catalogue, J. Paul Getty Museum, California, 1986), p. 68.
4. Susan Morgan (ed.), *Recollections of a Happy Life: Autobiography of Marianne North* (University Press of Virginia, 1993), p. 314.
5. Taylor, *Guests and Memories*, p. 227.
6. Troubridge, *Memories and Reflections*, p. 52.
7. Fuller and Hammersley, *Thackeray's Daughter*, p. 117.
8. *The Times*, 4 March 1879.
9. Brian Hinton, *Julia Margaret Cameron: Pioneer Victorian Photographer* (Isle of Wight, Julia Margaret Cameron Trust Ltd, 2001), p. 15.

BIBLIOGRAPHY

Allingham, H. and Radford, D. (eds), *William Allingham: A Diary*, Macmillan and Co., 1907.

Barrington, Mrs Russell, *G.F. Watts: Reminiscences*, George Allen, 1905.

Bird, N. *Tracing Echoes,* Wild Pansy Press, 2001.

Blunt, W. *England's Michelangelo: A Biography of George Frederic Watts*, Hamish Hamilton, 1975.

Boyd, E.F. 'The Pattle Sisters' MSS, Rutgers University, New Jersey, USA.

Cohen, M. (ed.), *The Letters of Lewis Carroll*, vol. 1, Macmillan, 1979.

—— *Lewis Carroll,* Macmillan, 1995.

Cohen, Sir H. *Indian and Home Memories*, Fisher Unwin, 1911.

Crawford, W. *The Keepers of Light: A History and Working Guide to Early Photographic Processes*, Morgan & Morgan, 1979.

Eden, E. *Up the Country*, R. Barnsley, 1866.

Emerson, P.H. *Naturalistic Photography*, Sampson Low, Marston, Searle & Rivington, 1890.

Fitzpatrick, K. *Lady Somerset*, Jonathan Cape, 1923.

Ford, C. *The Cameron Collection*, Van Nostrand Reinhold in association with the National Portrait Gallery, 1975.

Fuller, H.T. *Three Freshwater Friends: Tennyson, Watts and Mrs. Cameron*, Hunnyhill Publications, 2000.

—— and Hammersley, V. (eds), *Thackeray's Daughter*, Dublin: Euphorion Books, 1951.

Gernsheim, H. *Julia Margaret Cameron: Her Life and Photographic Work*, Gordon Fraser, 1975.

Gordon, C. *Beyond the Looking Glass*, Hodder & Stoughton, 1944.

Hamilton, V. (ed), *Annals of My Glasshouse: Photographs by Julia Margaret Cameron*, Ruth Chandler Williamson Gallery, Scripps College in association with University of Washington Press, 1996.

Bibliography

Hill, B. *Julia Margaret Cameron: A Victorian Family Portrait*, Peter Owen, 1973.

Hinton, B. *Immortal Faces: Julia Margaret Cameron on the Isle of Wight*, Isle of Wight County Press and Isle of Wight County Council, 2001.

—— *Julia Margaret Cameron: Pioneer Victorian Photographer*, Julia Margaret Cameron Trust Ltd, 2001.

Hoge, J.O. (ed.), *Lady Tennyson's Journal*, University Press of Virginia, 1981.

Hopkinson, A. *Julia Margaret Cameron*, Virago, 1986.

Ilchester, Earl of, *Chronicles of Holland House 1820–1900*, John Murray, 1937.

Jeffrey, I. *Photography: A Concise History*, Thames & Hudson, 1981.

Keene, H.G. *A Servant of 'John Company'*, W. Thacker & Co., 1987.

Marsh, J. *Christina Rossetti*, Jonathan Cape, 1994.

Martin, R.B. *Tennyson: The Unquiet Heart*, Faber & Faber, 1980.

Maas, J. *The Victorian Art World in Photographs*, Barrie & Jenkins, 1984.

Maitland, F.W. *The Life and Letters of Leslie Stephen*, Duckworth, 1906.

Monsarrat, A. *An Uneasy Victorian: Thackeray the Man*, New York, Dod, Mead & Company, 1980.

Morgan, S. (ed.), *Recollections of a Happy Life: Autobiography of Marianne North*, University Press of Virginia, 1993.

Noakes, V. *Edward Lear*, Fontana, 1979.

Powell, T. (ed.), *Victorian Photographs of Famous Men and Fair Women: Julia Margaret Cameron*, Hogarth Press, 1973.

Ritchie, H. (ed.), *Letters of Anne Thackeray Ritchie*, John Murray, 1924.

Ritchie, Lady, *From Friend to Friend*, John Murray, 1920.

Rosenblum, N. *A History of Women Photographers*, Abbeville Press, 1994.

Smyth, E. *Impressions that Remained*, Longman, Green & Co., 1919.

Strasser, A. *Victorian Photography*, Focal Press, 1942.

Taylor, H. *Autobiography*, vol. 2, Longman, Green & Co., 1885.

Taylor, U. *Guests and Memories*, Oxford University Press, 1924.

Tennyson, C. *Alfred Tennyson*, Macmillan, 1949.

Terry, E. *The Story of My Life*, Boydell Press, 1982.

Bibliography

Thwaite, A. *Emily Tennyson: The Poet's Wife*, Faber & Faber, 1996.

Troubridge, L. *Memories and Reflections*, Heinemann, 1925.

Ward, W. *Men and Matters*, Longman, 1914.

Watts, M.S. *George Frederic Watts*, Macmillan & Co., 1912.

Weaver, M. *Julia Margaret Cameron 1815–1879*, Herbert Press, 1984.

Weld, A.G. *Glimpses of Tennyson and of Some of his Relations and Friends*, Williams & Norgate, 1903.

Wheatcroft, A. *The Tennyson Album*, Routledge & Kegan Paul, 1980.

Wolf, S. *Julia Margaret Cameron's Women*, Yale University Press, 1957.

Woolf, V. *Freshwater: A Comedy*, Harcourt Inc., 1976.

INDEX

Index

Index

Index

Little Holland House 27–30, 31, 37, 38, 97

London 20–1, 22, 23
  International Exhibition 94, 97

Longfellow, Henry Wadsworth 76

Louis XVI of France 1

Macaulay, Thomas Babington 7

Mackenzie, Adeline (*née* Pattle) 2, 12

Mackenzie, Colin 12

Maclise, Daniel 39

Macmillan's Magazine 39, 87

Marie Antoinette, Queen 1–2

Marylebone church 17, 18

Maurice, Frederick Denison 92

Mill, John Stuart 82

Millais, John Everett 28, 81, 96

Milton, John 69, 92

Muhammad Phah Khan 12

Norman, Charles 40, 54

Norman, Julia (*née* Cameron) 10–11, 15 *bis*, 17, 40, 42, 54, 98

North, Marianne 111–12

Nunn, Pamela Gerrish 91

Ottington, Ellen 62, 113

Patmore, Coventry 28, 87

Pattle, Adeline (*née* de l'Etang; mother) 1, 2, 3, 5, 17, 18, 25

Pattle, Adeline (sister) *see* Mackenzie

Pattle, Harriet (sister) 2

Pattle, James (father) 1, 2, 3, 5, 25
  death and 'embalming' 17–18

Pattle, Louisa (sister) *see* Bayley

Pattle, Maria (sister) *see* Jackson

Pattle, Sarah (sister) *see* Prinsep

Pattle, Sophia (sister) *see* Dalrymple

Pattle, Virginia (sister) *see* Somers

Photographic News 76, 79, 81, 93

Photographic Notes 79

Photographic Society of London 79
  Journal 82, 83

Photographic Society of Scotland 81–2

Pre-Raphaelites 28, 30, 95–6

Prinsep, May 89, 90

Prinsep, Sarah (*née* Pattle) 2, 4, 5, 8, 18, 21–30 *passim*, 66–7, 67–8, 97, 109, 113–14

Prinsep, Thoby 8, 21, 22–3, 29, 67, 113–14

Prussia, Crown Prince of 75

Punch 26,

Putney Heath, house in 40, 43, 44, 51

Robinson, Henry Peach 81

Rossetti, Dante Gabriel 28, 39, 77, 96

Rossetti, William Michael 84, 99

Ruskin, John 28, 105

Ryan, Sir Edward 65, 85, 93, 98, 104

Ryan, Mary 47–8, 70

St Giles church, Camberwell 18

St Mary's church, Bogawantalawa 115

Schreiber, Lady Charlotte 30, 39

Shaw, George Bernard 88

Shepherd, Kate 62

Smyth, Ethel 5
  father quoted 17–18

Somers, Earl (Viscount Eastnor) 26, 62

Somers, Virginia, Countess (*née* Pattle) 2, 18, 22, 23, 25–6, 39, 106–7, 114

Index